Helping Adolescents and Adults to Build Self-Esteem

This book is due for return on or before the last date shown below.

By the same author

Helping Children to Build Self-Esteem
A Photocopiable Activities Book
Second Edition
Deborah M. Plummer
ISBN 978 1 84310 488 9
eISBN 978 1 84642 609 4

Self-Esteem Games for Children
Deborah M. Plummer
Illustrated by Jane Serrurier
ISBN 978 1 84310 424 7
eISBN 978 1 84642 574 5

Helping Children to Cope with Change, Stress and Anxiety
Deborah M. Plummer
Illustrated by Alice Harper
ISBN 978 1 84310 960 0
eISBN 978 0 85700 366 9

The Adventures of the Little Tin Tortoise
A Self-Esteem Story with Activities for Teachers, Parents and Carers
Deborah M. Plummer
ISBN 978 1 84310 406 3
eISBN 978 1 84642 465 6

of related interest

Banish Your Self-Esteem Thief
A Cognitive Behavioural Therapy Workbook on
Building Positive Self-Esteem for Young People
Kate Collins-Donnelly
ISBN 978 1 84905 462 1
eISBN 978 1 84905 462 1

Enhancing Self-Esteem
A Self-Esteem Training Package for Individuals with Disabilities
Nick Hagiliassis and Hrepsime Gulbenkoglu
ISBN 978 1 84310 353 0

Emotional Healing and Self-Esteem
Inner-life Skills of Relaxation, Visualisation
and Mediation for Children and Adolescents
Mark Pearson
ISBN 978 1 84310 224 3
eISBN 978 1 84642 437 3

Cool Connections with Cognitive Behavioural Therapy
Encouraging Self-esteem, Resilience and Well-being in
Children and Young People Using CBT Approaches
Laurie Seiler
ISBN 978 1 84310 618 0
eISBN 978 1 84642 765 7

Helping Adolescents and Adults to Build Self-Esteem

A Photocopiable Resource Book

Deborah M. Plummer

Illustrated by Alice Harper

Jessica Kingsley *Publishers*
London and Philadelphia

Material on activity sheets 5.1, 8.1, 8.8, 8.9 and Appendix A adapted with permission from *You Can Change – A Self-Help Guide to Managing Stress* (2003) by Diane Eaglen and Deborah Plummer. © Adult Speech and Language Therapy Service, Leicester 2003.

Some examples of Imagework exercises given in Chapter 3 and throughout Part II and also material in Appendix C on the Self-Esteem model for wellbeing originally appeared in Plummer, D. (2013) 'Stammering, Imagework and Self-Esteem.' In C. Cheasman, R. Everard and S. Simpson (eds) *Stammering Therapy from the Inside: New Perspectives on Working with Young People and Adults*. Guildford: J&R Press Ltd.

First published in 2004 by Jessica Kingsley Publishers

This second edition published in 2014
by Jessica Kingsley Publishers
73 Collier Street
London N1 9BE, UK
and
400 Market Street, Suite 400
Philadelphia, PA 19106, USA

www.jkp.com

Library of Congress Cataloging in Publication Data
A CIP catalog record for this book is available from the Library of Congress

British Library Cataloguing in Publication Data
A CIP catalogue record for this book is available from the British Library

ISBN 978 1 84905 425 6
eISBN 978 0 85700 794 0

Printed and bound in Great Britain

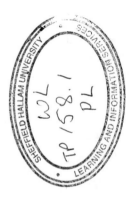

Contents

Acknowledgements

This book would not have been written without the generous support and inspirational teachings of several key people in my life. Dina Glouberman opened up the world of imagery for me and provided the nurturing environment necessary for my exploration of my subconscious mind. Her passion for her work generated a deep desire in me to further my experience and knowledge of Imagework through undergoing her practitioner training and teaching courses. I am grateful to Dina for reading and commenting on the original manuscript for the first edition of this book, adding to the ideas, and so generously sharing insights.

There have been many friends in the Imagework community who have also played an important part in this work. In particular, Hermione Elliott and Marsha Lomond, who have taught me so much about group facilitation by being such inspirational facilitators themselves.

Guy Shennan introduced me to the concepts of Solution Focused Brief Therapy and Pamela Gawler-Wright opened up further possibilities with her practitioner training course in Neurolinguistic Psychotherapy. Through example, and once again through their evident passion for their work, both Guy and Pam strengthened and enhanced my belief in the power of the subconscious and how this translates into the words and images that inform our 'self-talk' and our communications with others. This belief, of course, had its roots in my training as a speech and language therapist at University College, London. My tutors at UCL have therefore also played a part in the emergence of this book, particularly Renee Byrne, who taught me about Personal Construct Therapy and enthused me enough to complete further training in this field with Sharon Jackson. I am also grateful to Professor Jannet Wright. Her unstinting support and sound advice have been instrumental in keeping me writing through some difficult times.

There have been many others along the road – facilitators, tutors on counselling courses, clients, students, colleagues and friends – each contributing to my repertoire of activities and sparking new thoughts.

Stephen Jones, senior commissioning editor at Jessica Kingsley Publishers, has encouraged, enthused and gently suggested changes in direction at just the right times and in just the right proportions. This book is a 'sister' volume to *Helping Children to Build Self-Esteem*, which is also in its second edition. As I re-read the first manuscripts for both these books I realized what a sensitive and detailed job the editors at JKP have always done.

George Dunseth and Jane Serrurier have also read and re-read various incarnations of my work and have given invaluable advice and support.

Alice Harper has provided illustrations for this book; a qualified child counsellor herself, she is a constant reminder to me that healthy self-esteem is the foundation for an enriched and fulfilling life.

Introduction

Since writing the first edition of *Helping Adolescents and Adults to Build Self-Esteem* in 2005 I have had the fortunate opportunity to share my work with colleagues and students in higher education and to benefit from their feedback and engagement with many of the activities. The intervening years have also seen a continued growth in research within the neurosciences, leading to new insights into the workings of the brain. This has highlighted the enormous changes that take place during adolescence, and the plasticity of the brain throughout life. Alongside this there has been a burgeoning interest in both therapeutic and educational fields regarding the practice of mindfulness. It seems to be a useful time to update this book in order to integrate some of these aspects more fully.

As with the first edition, the suggested activities arise from a basis of carefully structured interactions and the strengthening of a set of 'foundation' elements for self-esteem. I have used terms related to the 'self' to distinguish each of the foundation elements: self-knowledge, self and others, self-acceptance, self-reliance, self-expression, self-confidence, self-awareness, and 'beyond self'.

This model acknowledges the relationship between the physical, social, emotional and spiritual aspects of our lives. It is firmly embedded in the concept of 'mutuality' (i.e. a balance between healthy connectedness with others and personal autonomy; see Harter 1999, page 295) and recognizes the importance of actual and perceived competence, and a strong sense of self-efficacy. The eight foundation elements are described in Part I, Chapter 1 'Self-Esteem and Wellbeing'. The information and activity sheets in Part II of this book are designed to enable participants to explore each element. Further explanation of the model can be found in Appendix C.

Whilst emphasis has been given to group work, the majority of activities are equally appropriate for work with individual clients or pupils, particularly where there is opportunity for structured support to aid the transfer of skills and strategies to a variety of situations relevant to that person's life. Most of the activities can easily be modified for discussion and practical application, without the need for worksheets, and are therefore suitable for participants who would prefer not to utilize written material. The 'relevant activities' and 'relevant information sheets' listed in the subject index illustrate the ways in which many of the activities in this book can be used for exploring more than one topic. Because of the potential for adaptation I have not given a specific age range for these activities. In their un-adapted form, they are generally geared towards older adolescents (15+) and adults. I would encourage you to be creative in using the material to suit your personal style and experience, and the needs, strengths and experiences of the adolescents and adults with whom you work. To help with this process, this second edition contains considerable additions to the facilitator notes and an expanded theory section.

Please note that throughout the text the pronouns 'he' and 'she' have been used interchangeably.

Part I

Theoretical and Practical Background

Chapter 1

Self-Esteem and Wellbeing

Self-esteem is a complex, multi-faceted aspect of life; a primary component in the building and maintenance of physical, emotional and spiritual wellbeing. The term 'healthy self-esteem' is often used in recognition of the fact that 'high' self-esteem may be (wrongly) seen as almost entirely based on feeling good about oneself. This could possibly be at the expense of other people's feelings. Healthy self-esteem is much more than simply feeling good about oneself. It encompasses feelings of actual and perceived competency and self-efficacy[1] and, most importantly, feelings of being lovable or 'approved' of. This includes self-approval and compassion towards oneself, as well as a sense of approval and warmth from others. Someone with healthy self-esteem is more likely to be self-motivated and self-reliant yet still understand the importance of mutuality and so be more likely to sustain respectful and fulfilling relationships with others. A person who has developed healthy self-esteem will be more able to make informed decisions. He will usually be more willing to try new ways of doing things, learning from mistakes and building confidence for future challenges. He will be able to recognize and develop his specific strengths and cope with changes successfully.

Self-esteem is undoubtedly a valuable psychological resource. Abraham Maslow, one of the founders of humanistic psychology, argued that not only is it necessary for wellbeing, but that the need for esteem is genetically a part

---

1   Albert Bandura defined self-efficacy as the *belief* that we are capable of doing something and that we can influence events that affect our lives (e.g. Bandura 1977). Bandura suggested that people who have perceptions of high self-efficacy often do better than those who have equal ability but less belief in themselves; they are more likely to persevere with difficult tasks and to use more effective problem-solving strategies; they also have a tendency to set themselves more demanding goals and to focus less on the possible consequences of failure. Bandura also showed how children internalize the standards of those adults who are important to them and how these standards then become self imposed. He argued that occasionally these self-controlled consequences of behaviour become more powerful than consequences from the external environment: 'there is no more devastating punishment than self-contempt' (Bandura 1971, page 28).

of us. Indeed, scientists have long known that genetics *do* play a part in the development and utilization of our psychological resources.

Neuro nugget

Recent studies (e.g. Saphire-Bernstein *et al.* 2011) appear to have identified a particular gene that is involved in the utilization of three important psychological resources for coping with stress and depression: mastery (the belief that one has control over one's own life), self-esteem and optimism. The gene in question is an oxytocin receptor. Oxytocin is a hormone known to aid the 'bonding' process after childbirth. It induces feelings of calmness and is also associated with empathy and positive social interactions. Levels of oxytocin vary enormously according to how much positive physical contact we experience.

However, while genes may predict behaviour, they do not determine it. Healthy self-esteem does not rely solely on genetics by any means – we also know that a nurturing environment is of primary importance. This, and the remarkable plasticity of the brain throughout life, coupled with our ability to think creatively and alter our perceptions, can lead to positive change, even when self-esteem resources have been debilitatingly low.

How, then, do we develop and maintain this vital aspect of our lives?

The link between self-esteem and self-concept

Self-esteem has its roots in the development of our *self-concept*: the overall view that we have of ourselves. R.B. Burns describes the self-concept as 'a composite image of what we think we are, what we think we can achieve, what we think others think of us and what we would like to be' (Burns 1979, page xx). Developmental psychologist Susan Harter prefers the term 'self-representations', which she defines as 'attributes or characteristics of the self that are consciously acknowledged by the individual through language – that is, how one describes oneself' (Harter 1999, page 3). In essence, then, our self-concept is the internal 'word' and 'picture' image that we have of ourselves at any given time.

We generally try to act in a way that fits in with our self-concept. When new information is received to add to our system of beliefs about ourselves we are likely to 'filter out' the bits that we think are not relevant to us. If the information fits in with our self-concept we will probably accept it as being true (even if it is not based on any factual evidence). If it is not consistent with how we see ourselves then we might ignore it, misinterpret it or reject it completely. In this way our beliefs affect the way we see the world and this, in turn, informs our behaviour.

Self-evaluation

An important aspect of healthy self-esteem is the way in which individuals *evaluate* their self-concept, usually in comparison with an *ideal self*. As Harter points out, it is important to also distinguish between

self-evaluations that represent global characteristics of the individual (e.g., 'I am a worthwhile person') and those that reflect the individual's sense of adequacy across particular domains such as one's cognitive competence (e.g., 'I am smart'), social competence (e.g., 'I am well liked by peers'), athletic competence (e.g., 'I am good at sports') and so forth. (Harter 1999, page 5)

The extent to which a person's self-evaluations in different areas of life affects her global sense of self-worth and self-efficacy will depend on the level of importance she places on each area at any one time.

Self-evaluation is heavily influenced by the way in which we perceive other people's reactions to what we do and say: we look to the significant people in our lives (parents, grandparents, teachers, etc.) to show us that we are loved and approved of, and this process begins with our earliest interactions as babies: 'The infant needs to be able to discover his/her capacity to light up the mother's face — for here is to be found the fundamental basis of… self-esteem' (Casement 1990, page 93).

Neuro nugget

The quality of early infant-parent bonding and the formation of secure attachments have long been recognized as a major factor in the development of a healthy self-concept and feelings of self-worth and competency (e.g. Bowlby 1969; Ainsworth, Bell and Stayton 1971; Main and Solomon 1990). Such influences include the ability of carers to tune into their child's feelings and provide the comfort and touch which allows the emotion-regulation system to develop and to function effectively. Where this natural process is inhibited there may be long-term consequences. Research neuroscientist Lise Eliot, for example, cites a study undertaken by researchers at the University of Washington who compared frontal-lobe EEG measures in the infants of depressed and non-depressed mothers. They found that by about one year of age, babies whose mothers were depressed showed a different pattern of neural responsiveness than control babies. During playful interactions, they experienced less activation of the left hemisphere (the 'feel-good' side) than control babies (Eliot 1999).

Studies have also shown that four-year-olds who have been brought up in highly stressful environments have a measurably smaller pre-frontal cortex compared to four-year-olds who have experienced a nurturing environment. These children show clear signs of lack of social competence, an inability to manage stress and the inability to see things from another child's viewpoint (Gerhardt 2004).

The interplay between self-concept and self-evaluation affects not only the levels, but also the stability of self-esteem – the more that we invest our feelings of self-worth in 'everyday outcomes' (such as experiencing difficulty in a familiar situation which we consider should be 'easy' for most people) and the less well-developed our self-concepts, the more unstable our self-esteem is likely to be (Greenier, Kernis and Waschull 1995, page 67).

If a child's early experiences have been primarily positive with regard to the building of self-esteem then eventually he will be able to internalize the feelings of self-worth and rely less and less on others for approval and confirmation that he is OK. A child who remains dependent on external sources for the maintenance of self-esteem, however, will find life's difficulties harder to handle: 'Such a child will develop into an adult who will continue to feel that he has to be successful, or good, or approved of by everyone, if he is to retain any sense of his own value' (Storr 1989, page 96). So, chronic low self-esteem may be a product of genetic predisposition, personal resources, childhood experiences and belief patterns. Feelings of self-worth and competency can also be temporarily affected when we are feeling particularly vulnerable, such as after the loss of a loved one, a change in work circumstances, redundancy or long-term illness. This vulnerability is also often apparent at major life stages, for example, moving from being dependent on our parents to being independent; starting a family of our own; entering the renowned 'mid-life' period or reaching old age, when our roles may be changing yet again. For some people, such changes affect the way that they have always defined themselves (partner, parent, provider, decision-maker, expert) and with this loss or blurring of roles comes a loss of self-esteem. Whilst most of us would be affected to some degree by these changes, for those who have little or no internal resources such events can have an even greater impact.

Adolescence and self-esteem

Adolescence (the period between puberty and adulthood) is generally recognized as a particularly difficult time of uncertainty and feelings of vulnerability. As youngsters enter this turbulent time of life they are usually experiencing heightened self-awareness and are embroiled in the struggle to re-invent or rediscover the 'real' self:

He is not yet someone with a set appearance or with an identity which has been tested in the society around him…As the sense of self is so much at the centre of questions for the adolescent, it is no wonder that he makes it a focus of preoccupation. (Rayner 1993, page 157)

The young adolescent may be mourning the passing of childhood, however much he may want to be more 'grown up'. Part of this process may involve him deliberately alienating others, particularly family. It is a time when peers become increasingly important and play a vital role in helping him to define himself and to build his self-esteem as an independent person. He will often idealize others (such as celebrities, teachers or older adolescents). At the same time, although he may want independence, he also has the need for nurture and friendship. Sexuality becomes more of a major concern and can be a primary source of jealousy and low self-esteem. He is often full of doubts about how others view him, about where he 'fits in' to the greater scheme of life and about the reality of his thoughts.

In addition to all this, the adolescent brain is undergoing huge physical changes, particularly in the frontal cortex, that part of the brain responsible for such things as reasoning, decision-making, problem-solving and assessing risk (see page 93's 'neuro nugget'). It is little wonder that this can so often be a time of 'crisis' and low self-esteem.

What happens if self-esteem is low?

The link between low self-esteem and adolescent suicides has been well documented. In a study involving adolescent psychiatric inpatients and high school students Overholser and colleagues concluded that low self-esteem was closely related to higher levels of depression, hopelessness, suicidal ideation, and an increased likelihood of having previously attempted suicide (Overholser *et al.* 1995).

Low self-esteem has also been linked to adolescent use and abuse of alcohol and drugs, adolescent pregnancy and unprotected sexual encounters (e.g. California Task Force 1990; Harper and Marshall 1991).

Adolescents and adults with low self-esteem will invariably have problems in forming close attachments, partly because it is often so difficult for them to believe themselves worthy of a fulfilling relationship with another person. Low self-esteem can also lead to anxiety and confusion so that misunderstandings can easily occur and there is a tendency to do a lot more biased 'filtering' (see page 80), leading to a distorted view of self and others. People with low self-esteem may act in a very passive way or may be aggressive, quick to get in first before they themselves are attacked, rejecting others before they are rejected.

They tend to place little value on their abilities and often deny their successes. They find it difficult to set goals and to problem-solve. Self-confidence is reduced and there is an unwillingness to try because of fear of failure. Consequently, they may perform well below their academic and social capabilities. They invariably begin to expect the worst in life and their self-limiting beliefs become a self-fulfilling prophecy.

There are also many people who *do* achieve at or near their potential but have a constant fear of failure and a drive for perfection that may preclude creativity and experimentation. Such a person may set unrealistically high goals for himself, thus constantly confirming to himself that he is 'no good' each time he experiences failure.

A self-esteem approach to wellbeing

Fortunately, there is much that can be done to build and maintain self-esteem. In more extreme cases, the effects of neglect or lack of loving relationships during babyhood will undoubtedly complicate the process but every one of us does have a remarkable capacity for growth and change and, as Virginia Satir suggests:

Since the feeling of worth has been learned, it can be unlearned, and something new can be learned in its place. The possibility for this learning lasts from birth to death, so it is never too late. At any point in a person's life he can begin to feel better about himself. (Satir 1991, page 27)

My observations and clinical experience indicate that as we grow through childhood into adolescence and beyond, there are eight 'foundation elements' that increasingly contribute to healthy self-esteem and thereby lead to social and emotional wellbeing. I believe that the interaction is reciprocal – healthy levels of self-esteem will enable the consolidation and growth of these elements. I also see them as closely inter-dependent. Although there will be times when some areas may be more central to a person's stage of life and needs than others, I believe that it is important to explore all eight elements in order to help individuals to establish (or re-establish) and maintain healthy self-esteem and general wellbeing.

The key features of these elements involve: *developing, knowing, recognizing, believing, feeling* and *understanding*. The information and activity sheets in Part II of this book are designed to enable participants to explore each element. The eight elements are outlined below. Further details of this model can be found in Appendix C.

The eight foundation elements for healthy self-esteem
Self-knowledge *(see Part II, Section 3: 'Who Am I?)*

Development of this foundation element contributes to the building of an 'awakened' relationship with the self. Self-knowledge involves:

- developing a sense of security in terms of a strong sense of self: an understanding of who 'I' am and where I fit into the social world around me

- developing and maintaining my personal values — my guiding principles in life

- understanding differences and commonalities — how I am different from others in looks and character and how I can also have things in common with others

- knowing that I have many aspects to my personality

- developing a sense of my personal history — my own 'life story'.

Self-awareness (see Part II, Section 4: 'Self-Awareness' and Section 5: 'The Challenge of Change')

Self-awareness is the cornerstone of realistic self-evaluation. It involves:

- developing the ability to be focused in the 'here and now' rather than absorbed in negative thoughts about the past or future — this includes an awareness of my feelings as they arise

- understanding that emotional, mental and physical changes are a natural part of my life

- being aware of the normal fluctuations in how I feel and how these link to my thoughts and behaviour; recognizing that I have choices about how I think, feel and behave

- knowing what I am capable of, and learning to set realistic yet challenging goals

- developing and maintaining emotional intelligence.[2]

Self-acceptance (see Part II, Section 6: 'Self-Acceptance')

This involves:

- knowing my own strengths and recognizing areas that I find difficult and may want to work on

---

2   Daniel Goleman suggests that emotional intelligence involves the ability to recognize and understand our own emotions and those of others, the ability to manage our emotions effectively and the ability to motivate ourselves (Goleman 1996, pages 43–4). Emotional intelligence within this model of self-esteem, therefore, also includes self-reliance (foundation element 4) and links with foundation element 2: self and others.

- accepting that it is natural to make mistakes and that this is sometimes how we learn best

- feeling OK about my physical body and enhancing positive body awareness so that I can, for example, let go of unwanted tension or focus on calm breathing (see focusing exercise on page 261).

Self and others (see Part II, Section 7: 'Self and Others')

This involves:

- understanding the joys and challenges of relationships: learning to trust and to negotiate and cooperate with others; being able to see things from another person's perspective (empathy) and developing an understanding of how they might see me; learning respect and tolerance for other people's needs and views

- developing the capacity to recognize and accept helpful feedback from others

- developing and maintaining my own identity as a separate person while still recognizing the natural mutuality and interdependence of relationships

- developing a sense of my family/cultural 'story'.

Self-reliance (see Part II, Section 8: 'Self-Reliance and Managing Stress')

This involves:

- knowing how to take care of myself, both physically and emotionally

- building a measure of independence, emotional resilience and self-motivation; believing that I have mastery over my life and can meet challenges as and when they arise

- reducing my reliance on other people's opinions and evaluations.

Self-expression (see Part II, Section 9: 'Self-Expression')

This involves:

- understanding that my interactions reflect my beliefs about myself and about others

- building and maintaining a sense of enjoyment and effectiveness in the act of communication

- developing creativity in self-expression and recognizing and celebrating the unique and diverse ways in which we each express who we are.

Self-confidence (see Part II, Section 10: 'Creative Problem-Solving')

This involves:

- developing a strong sense of self-efficacy

- knowing that my opinions, thoughts and actions have value and that I have the right to express them

- developing my knowledge and skills so that I feel able to experiment with different methods of problem-solving and can be flexible enough to alter my strategies if needed

- feeling strong enough to accept challenges and make choices

- feeling secure enough in myself to be able to cope with the unexpected.

Beyond self (relevant to all sections in Part II)

This involves:

- deepening my awareness and engagement with other people, with life and with my inner self (this might manifest in a number of ways such as a strong sense of connection with music, art, or the wonders of the universe; or a transpersonal/spiritual element which may or may not be based in religious beliefs)

- developing an ability to focus and reflect upon realities beyond 'the self'

- acceptance of living with a degree of uncertainty and 'not knowing' in life

- developing my ability to imagine.

The process of building self-esteem can have unsought for and surprising repercussions in many areas of life. In some instances this can be as far-reaching as a reconfiguration of the whole self-concept, while for others it may simply involve a deeper understanding of their relationship with their inner world and perhaps lead to 'a quiet pleasure in being one's self' (Rogers 1961, page 87). The next chapter therefore explores aspects of change in the context of a self-esteem approach to wellbeing.

Suggestions for further reading

Gerhardt, S. (2004) *Why Love Matters: How Affection Shapes a Baby's Brain.* London: Routledge.

Harter, S. (1999) *The Construction of the Self.* New York: Guilford Press.

Maslow, A.H. (1962) *Toward a Psychology of Being.* Princeton, NJ: Van Nostrand.

Plummer, D. (2007) *Helping Children to Build Self-Esteem* (second edition). London: Jessica Kingsley Publishers.

Rayner, E. (1993) *Human Development: An Introduction to the Psychodynamics of Growth, Maturity and Ageing.* London: Routledge.

Satir, V. (1991) *Peoplemaking.* London: Souvenir Press.

Storr, A. (1989) *Solitude.* London: Fontana.

Chapter 2

Self-Esteem, Learning and the Process of Change

One of my earliest realizations as a speech and language therapist was the importance and value of healthy self-esteem in the process of change. It was evident that those who were self-aware and able to evaluate their self-concept realistically were much more likely to make long-lasting changes in their relationship with their communication difficulties. It was also clear that the prospect of change, whether through therapy or self-help, can be daunting for many people, however 'healthy' their levels of self-esteem might be.

Having some sort of framework can help to provide a sense of direction and to give an overview of what is happening as the process unfolds. Personal construct theory (PCT) offers one such framework. Elements of this theory have informed many of the activities in Part II of this book.

In the 1950s American psychologist George Kelly outlined a theory of personal development which we can use to look at how we make sense of our world and how we deal with change as individuals (Kelly 1955). Kelly suggested that each of us is a 'scientist' – a seeker of patterns and a hypothesis tester. He said that we test out our hypotheses (what we believe about ourselves and the world) by making experiments throughout life. Sometimes these experiments validate our hypotheses and so strengthen our belief system. Sometimes our experiments don't turn out the way we expected, so we either alter our beliefs or alter our experiment. By doing this we have the potential to constantly 'reinvent' ourselves.

As we continue to make our experiments we find patterns in how the world operates and in how we operate within the world. Because we can see certain similarities and contrasts in what is happening in our environment we begin to anticipate events, to predict outcomes. Kelly called the basis of these anticipations 'constructs'. For example, I may have a construct day/night. I know from experience that one follows the other and that they have different characteristics such as light/dark. I can therefore predict or anticipate that this will always be the case. All constructs have a contrasting element; we can't know what 'day' is if we don't have 'night' to contrast it with.

Constructs are linked together to form a hierarchical structure, and in this way the use of one construct (because it is part of a system) implies the relevance of several others. To take the example of day and night again, one association I might have with day is 'work' and for 'night' I might also have a construct of 'sleep'. Of course, for other people this might be reversed or night could subsume the construct 'restless', and so on.

It follows that a person's constructs about themselves and about the world around them will have a profound effect on how they behave and relate to others.

The context in which constructs are used is vital and we can never assume that we know exactly what other people mean by certain constructs unless we explore it with them in more depth. One way of doing this is to find out what their opposite (personal contrast) is for a given construct. Let's say that Person A has low self-esteem. She considers herself to be 'painfully shy', and her opposite of this is 'outgoing'. She wants to become more outgoing and explores what it would be like to change in this direction by elaborating her construct of outgoing to see what that would involve. Person B also considers herself to be shy. Her opposite of 'shy' is 'conceited'. She has no wish to make changes in this direction and sees 'shy' as a predominantly positive characteristic. However, once she elaborates her construct of shy and its contrast she realizes that it does imply some other constructs which are not so agreeable to her. Exploring or 'elaborating' the contrasting element of a construct can help to show the way forward.

Also, trying to stop doing one thing without first elaborating an alternative doesn't usually work very successfully. Imagine saying to yourself 'Don't get anxious!' The image that you will have in your mind will be of yourself being in an anxious state, and this is very likely to trigger the actual feelings of anxiety. If you are able to elaborate your personal opposite of anxious and you can imagine this vividly enough, you will have a better sense of what that more desirable state entails. In this case, knowing what you are aiming for helps you to stop doing what you don't want! (See Chapter 3, 'Working with Imagery and the Imagination'.)

Kelly said that a person's construct system provides both freedom and constraint; the system is ever-changing, but at any one time we are limited to making choices within the structure we have invented for ourselves. We do not need to be the victim of our past, however, as there are always other pathways along which we can move so as to see ourselves in a new light.

So, according to this theory of development, when we look at what we would like to change in our lives we also need to look at some of the other constructs we have which might be affected by this change or which might be preventing us from changing. We then need to explore or elaborate the opposite side of the construct. If I want to be more outgoing, what exactly does outgoing consist of?

What makes change difficult?

Familiarity

Any change in beliefs, thoughts or behaviours automatically entails having to give something up. As well as the positive intention to change therefore, there will often also be uncertainty and possibly some resistance. This resistance centres on letting go of what is most familiar to us. This can prove difficult – we can at least continue to predict outcomes if we stay with an old belief or behaviour.

Threat

Kelly defined threat as the awareness of an imminent 'comprehensive' change in our central or 'core' constructs. Our core constructs are the most resistant to change because they define the essence of how we see ourselves, the most important aspects of how we make sense of the world. We don't want this change to happen so we may try to avoid or sabotage the change. Threat is extremely uncomfortable. A person who feels under threat in this way may experience the sensations associated with panic or anger. This can sometimes be triggered by seemingly small events. Someone with low self-esteem who has purposefully developed a caring role in her relationships and sees this as central to her identity may, for example, react with disproportionate panic at the prospect of attempting to be more assertive with someone who is taking advantage of her caring nature.

Fear

This is described as an awareness of an imminent but smaller change. It is not as strong a feeling as threat but can still be disagreeable!

Anxiety

Kelly described anxiety as the awareness that the events with which we are confronted lie outside the 'range of convenience' of our construct system. In other words, the event has not been part of our previous experience so we can't accurately predict what is going to happen. We basically don't know what to do. Anxiety is fed by avoidance. If we don't experiment with our beliefs and behaviours we will continue to keep our world small and manageable, avoiding changes and becoming more and more anxious. The more we avoid, the more anxious we become, because we have no experience from which we can predict possible outcomes. Kelly argued that the way to overcome these feelings is to actively 'experiment' so that we can increase the range of our experiences. There may be many activities within a self-esteem course which are new to participants. Seeing these as 'experiments' which can be carried out within the group before attempting them with others can help individuals to assimilate changes more comfortably.

Guilt

Another obstacle to change is the feeling of guilt. Kelly described guilt feelings as arising when we feel we are about to step, or have already stepped, outside the 'core' role structure that we have invented for ourselves. For example, if my core role is mother and this role subsumes constructs such as caring, available and loving, I am likely to feel guilt if I then step out of this role for the first time in order to go back to work and I see my caring and loving constructs as being compromised by my 'availability'. This will be especially true if some of my 'work' constructs are in direct opposition to those of 'mother'.

Guilt feelings can be very destructive. They go with the language of 'I should, I ought, I must' and may lead once again to avoidance of change. In order to overcome guilt we may need to 'reframe' the change, look at it from other aspects, elaborate our new role or reach a compromise in order to make the change more manageable for ourselves.

Hostility

Hostility is the continued effort to find evidence in support of something that clearly isn't valid. This may result in trying to manipulate people and events in order to get the results that you want.

Threat, fear, anxiety, guilt and hostility are known as constructs of transition. The feelings they encapsulate are not mutually exclusive and can be experienced to different degrees. They provide a useful indicator as to why changes in how we are or in how we see ourselves can sometimes be difficult. Recognition of these feelings can also provide us with a positive tool for moving on; there are always other options open to us, other experiments that we can make.

Having attended several courses on personal construct theory as part of my professional training, I felt that I had a far better understanding of some of my own difficulties in making the changes that I desired in life, but I wanted something further to balance out the logical aspects of this approach. My search eventually led me to Imagework. Imagework contains many of the elements of personal construct theory and offers a creative way of using our natural imaginative abilities to enhance our wellbeing and to cope with life's challenges. Both personal construct theory and Imagework look beyond *what* we think to *how* we think and what we *experience*. Use of the imagination is explored further in the next chapter and is an important element of the activities throughout this book.

Suggestions for further reading

Dalton, P. and Dunnett, G. (2005) *A Psychology for Living: Personal Construct Theory for Professionals and Clients* (second edition). Chichester: John Wiley and Sons.

Fransella, F. and Dalton, P. (1990) *Personal Construct Counselling in Action*. London: Sage.

Kelly, G.A. (1955) *The Psychology of Personal Constructs*. New York: Norton.

Chapter 3

Working with Imagery and the Imagination

The ability to imagine is an important aspect of learning, creativity and problem-solving. It is also vital for empathy: the ability to see things from another person's point of view and to be aware of other's needs. Imagination allows us to be more effective in directing our attention both internally (to images, feelings and thoughts) and externally to our environment and to other people. Imagination is the key to effective change.

What are images?

What images do you have when you think of the following?

- a waterfall cascading down a mountainside

- a freshly mown lawn

- stroking a cat

- waiting at a busy railway station

- attending an important interview.

Which was your strongest sense – touch, sight, sound, smell? Were you aware of any emotions associated with the images? Perhaps you experienced a mixture of all these things but to varying degrees. Whatever you saw, felt, heard or smelled was, of course, in your imagination and the strength of each of your images will have been due, in part, to your previous experiences and memories. For example, someone whose main experiences of railway stations are of saying goodbye to loved ones is likely to have very different feelings or 'energy' connected with their images compared to someone who travels a great deal for pleasure and has a sense of excitement associated with train journeys. A freshly mown lawn could conjure up memories of pleasant summers or it could perhaps engender feelings of discomfort associated with allergies.

In this way, even if two people have the same image they will *experience* it very differently; each person's imagery is unique to them. This element of uniqueness in images also means that both stored and newly created images come in many forms. Although many people find that they can 'see' things in their imagination this is by no means the case for everyone. Some people may get a 'sense' of an image but not a clear picture. They may be more aware of the sound or smell or feeling associated with it. None of these experiences are 'better' than another and no matter how we experience images it is possible to train ourselves to become more aware of them and to create new ones for ourselves.

In the above examples you were bringing stored images into your imagination through choice. Images can also surface from the unconscious when we are least expecting them! For example, have you ever felt uncomfortable with someone for no obvious reason? It may be that they 'remind' you of an unpleasant encounter with someone else, even though you are not consciously aware of this connection. Similarly, you may have experienced the effects of the unconscious when you have suddenly felt angry or sad about something and wondered 'Where did that come from?' or 'It's not like me to get upset over that!' Of course, pleasant feelings can also be evoked by unconscious associations — a sound, a smell, or perhaps the sight of a certain object may trigger a feeling of happiness, contentment and so on because of its link with past events. The imagination can also directly affect your body. For example it affects the autonomic nervous system — that part of our nervous system that controls such things as heart rate, breathing, circulation, body temperature and digestive processes. How can images affect such a complex system? If I tell myself to increase my heart rate or sweat then I'm not likely to notice much response! But if I imagine a frightening event or am anticipating a difficult situation like giving a presentation then my body will respond accordingly.

Because of the perpetual interaction between mind, body and emotions if I believe something about myself strongly enough I am likely to experience it in my life in actuality. If I believe that I am 'shy' or 'clumsy' then I will have a picture of myself in different situations acting in a 'shy' or 'clumsy' way. I will not be projecting a positive image of myself onto future events and I will feel and act in the way that I imagined, so continuing to reaffirm this picture of myself. In other words, telling myself how badly I am going to do in some activity may in fact lead to actual poor performance — my imagination results in a self-fulfilling prophecy.

Neuro nugget

The plasticity of the brain and the way in which it can form new neuronal connections is well documented. It has been found that new connections can be formed simply by imagining doing something over and over again. In this way, the imagination can affect actual ability, such as learning to play the piano or to play golf.

Constructive use of the imaginative process is a vital part of a child's development and yet, as we grow into adulthood, the majority of us start to lose touch with this ability. We relegate the imagination to times of daydreaming and discourage our children with such comments as 'don't be silly, it's only your imagination'. It seems that for most of us the imagination eventually becomes synonymous with things that are 'different' from, and perhaps compensate for, the realities of life but which are unlikely to ever come true for us. This belief is reflected in some of the following definitions of the imagination given to me by a group of teenagers:

'Pictures and stories and dreams that you form in your head.' Chloe, 16

'Something that thinks things up the way you want them, not the way they are.' Ruppa, 16

'The part of you that can make up anything you want.' Stuart, 17

'Where your best things happen to you.' Sharon, 16

'A place where bad things don't happen.' Katie, 16

'A place inside you where all your dreams are kept.' Frances, 15

It is surely time to rectify this situation since the tools are available to help us to realize some of our 'internal dreams'. Imagework can play an important part in this realization. By using the power of the imagination in a positive way, each one of us can begin to alter our personal futures and promote our own development towards confidence and wellbeing.

What is Imagework?

The term Imagework was conceived by Dr Dina Glouberman who leads Imagework courses internationally. Imagework involves 'developing the receptive ability to tune into the images that guide us, and the active ability to create new images that enhance our health, happiness, and creativity' (Glouberman 2003, page 6).

The process requires the ability to focus on a particular feeling, problem, dilemma, puzzle or question and then to enter a period of relaxation, allowing images to 'emerge' from the unconscious which somehow represent the area to be explored, without any attempt to consciously construct them. The imagination then acts like a 'meeting place' between the conscious and unconscious mind, a 'common ground where both meet on equal terms and create a life experience that combines the elements of both' (Johnson 1989).

The imageworker (explorer) then works with the images, either alone or with a guide, in order to gain a better understanding of their meaning and relevance in his life. The interactions are structured in such a way as to facilitate insight without any presuppositions and prejudices. In other words, as with other forms of active imagination, Imagework starts from the premise that the unconscious has its own wisdom. Although the person is consciously engaged in the process (i.e. it does not involve deep hypnosis), he allows his imagination to flow where it wants and then works with whatever images arise:

[T]he images that come in this way have a powerful ability to sum up with a telling metaphor the basic structure of whatever it is you are asking about. The metaphor tends to be so accurate that the more you explore it, the more it can be seen to correspond on every level and in every detail not only with the specific problem but even with your life as a whole. The implicit becomes suddenly explicit, the complexities of the problem become streamlined into a simple structure, the history of the situation becomes obvious, and suddenly a resolution emerges where it seemed impossible before. (Glouberman 2003, page 91)

Imagework also allows us to explore our present reality from the *perspective* of our images: to experience the image by 'stepping into it' or 'becoming it'. The image is further expanded and deepened through active dialogue and, where appropriate, it may be transformed or replaced.

So, for example, if I ask you to allow an image to emerge that somehow represents how you are feeling right now, each reader will of course see, hear or sense something different (remember, images do not have to be visual). As I am writing this I am sensing a baby dragon trying to stretch its wing – I have a pain in my shoulder that is aggravating me and I am finding it difficult to write. When I allow myself a moment to step into being the baby dragon I am keen to tell my 'self' (Deborah, sitting at the computer) that, although I am just a baby pain, I have the potential to cause aggravation to others by becoming more dragon-like unless I am soothed. I know immediately that this is not just about me dealing with discomfort before it gets worse. I can get very 'tetchy' and breathe fire when I am tired or in pain! I have a short talk with the baby dragon. I tell it that I am going to take a break in a few minutes and I make a note to take my awareness of potential 'tetchyness' with me so that I do not allow it to affect my interactions with my family. I sense the baby dragon settling into a more relaxed state – still there, but more calm.

The idea of working with images from the unconscious is not new, of course. It played an important part in the healing traditions of many ancient cultures and has been particularly well documented in the work of Austrian psychoanalyst, Carl Jung, and in the subsequent work of psychotherapists such as Robert Johnson (e.g. Johnson 1989) and James Hillman (e.g. Hillman 1990). The exploration of personal imagery is now an established basis of many forms of therapy and counselling.

The richness and creativity of our unconscious mind and the abundance of images available to us mean that we not only have the opportunity to understand ourselves more fully and make more informed choices in life, but also to create new images that will work for us. These can replace or outweigh old stored images, formed through past experience, that are no longer useful for our self-development. Carl Jung, for example, described the unconscious as:

a living psychic entity which, it seems, is relatively autonomous, behaving as if it were a personality with intentions of its own… Completely new thoughts and creative ideas can present themselves from the unconscious – thoughts that have never been conscious before. They grow up from the dark depths of the mind like a lotus and form a most important part of the subliminal psyche. (Jung 1978, page 25)

We have all experienced these 'creative ideas' though we may not have been aware of using any specific technique to access them. For example, when a problem seems unsolvable, switching conscious attention away from it and involving yourself in some other activity (going for a walk perhaps) can often result in a solution suddenly 'coming to mind'. Perhaps you have had the experience of solving a problem during dreaming or while meditating. You may have found that you have had sudden flashes of inspiration when you are practising relaxation techniques. The more deeply relaxed you are in both mind and body, the more likely this is to happen.

Robert Johnson also describes how by talking to our images and interacting with them we will invariably find that 'they tell you things you never consciously knew and express thoughts that you never consciously thought' (Johnson 1989, page 138). Time and time again, when I have introduced Imagework to students and clients, including those who are sceptical and feel that they 'won't be able to get an image', the unconscious processes reveal themselves in all their glory. Sometimes this manifests in very obvious metaphors, sometimes in ways that require further exploration in order to contribute to a more meaningful experience.

Hillman suggests that we do not necessarily need to interpret the images that arise, but that the image itself is more important, more inclusive and more complex than what we have to say about it (see, for example, Hillman

1990). This means that we should also never try to interpret images for someone else. The guide can, however, ask questions in order to help the imageworker come to their own understanding, and certainly once an image or set of images have been worked with for a while, it is often possible for the imageworker to make a tentative mapping onto actual life. She may then experience an 'aha' sensation ("That feels right") which leads to a shift in perception and opens up possibilities for movement and change.

Conversational Imagework

Yet another way in which we can engage in Imagework is through heightening our awareness of metaphors used during conversations. A person may, for example, talk about the experience of feeling under-confident as being akin to being in a cage or a cave. Rather than just exploring the fact of being trapped, imagining becoming the image of the cave or cage can lead to a deeper understanding of the relationship between the person and his experience of confidence.

Kim referred to her sudden loss of confidence in social situations as being like falling into a deep hole. The hole was muddy and slippery; she was trying to climb out but was making no headway. When she imagined being the hole she realized that it wasn't actually as big as she had thought. The mud was indeed slippery but that meant that the hole 'felt' impermanent and transformable. It was quite concerned that Kim was 'thrashing about' so much and making things worse! 'Slow and steady' was the message she received from this image.

Images and associative sensitivity

A well-developed imagination can also lead us to be so in tune with another person that we may find ourselves entering into a shared space, where what is happening is no longer simply a function of 'their imagination' and 'my imagination' as separate processes, but is instead an interactive and dynamic experience which results in the emergence of new and often deeply meaningful images. So, for example, you may be engrossed in listening to someone's personal story about a dilemma or problem and find that an image comes to mind which at first does not seem to be connected to the words that the other person is actually using. Taking the step to share this image can have a profound effect. The other person may have an immediate and deep sense of 'being heard' — 'Yes, that's *exactly* how it is' or 'I hadn't realized, but that makes so much sense to me'.

This phenomenon has been extensively described by Cox and Theilgaard who refer to this level of attunement as a form of 'associative sensitivity' and, although working in the field of psychotherapy and psychiatry, they suggest that such sensitivity is not confined to the clinical field alone:

Indeed it enhances all deep human encounters. We found that an image could safely hold experience which was too painful, too brittle, or too broken to be firm enough to tolerate analysis. Such patients enabled us to see that the image, activated by metaphor, could be the location of exploration or the fabric of support. (Cox and Theilgaard 1987, page xiii)

I have also observed this sensitivity and attunement to others many times amongst groups of people who have begun to know each other well, to the extent that sometimes a group member will say with great conviction 'I think I have someone else's image' and, sure enough, they do!

Summary

Although Imagework is evidently unsuitable for people who are not firmly grounded in reality, it is perfectly possible to engage with imagery and the workings of the unconscious at a level that 'makes sense' without delving into the depths that might perhaps be explored between a psychotherapist and his or her clients. This is not about uncovering buried traumas and defences, but rather about facilitating those 'aha' moments that help people to move forward with their understanding of themselves and with their aspirations. It can be an incredibly powerful and life-changing process. As with any personal development tool, participants need to experience safety and understand the images as metaphors – they represent the truth for us *as we see it at the time*, within the story that we are telling ourselves – they are not fixed entities.

Providing a person with the means to foster creative use of the imagination can help them to build a unified sense of their inner and outer worlds; can enable them to see events, problems, and challenges from a different viewpoint; and can help them to find the way forward that is most appropriate for their individual needs. The resultant ability to make more informed choices in life will surely lead to a feeling of control, more effective learning, more fulfilling relationships and greater self-esteem. In fact, the imagination is a natural resource that none of us can afford to ignore!

Suggestions for further reading

Glouberman, D. (2010) *Life Choices, Life Changes: Develop your Personal Vision with Imagework.* London: Skyros Books.

Johnson, R.A. (1989) *Inner Work: Using Dreams and Active Imagination for Personal Growth.* New York: HarperSanFrancisco.

Jung, C.G. (1978) (ed.) *Man and His Symbols.* London: Pan Books (Picador edition).

Chapter 4

Learning and Generalizing Knowledge and Skills

Encouraging self-help

From the very start of a course of this nature, facilitators need to keep in mind strategies for promoting self-help skills. Progress towards increased self-motivation and maintenance of healthy self-esteem is greatly enhanced when a person has had ample experience of identifying his own needs and working out his own solutions to his difficulties. As facilitators we can offer the space, time and possible strategies for this learning to take place, but it is also crucial to build in more and more 'do at home' activities and chances for group members to facilitate each other.

Supporting someone in building their self-esteem must inevitably involve some assumptions on our part. If we make these assumptions transparent to them then we can encourage the 'go it alone' element in a variety of ways.

Most obviously we can make it clear that we believe that everyone is capable of facilitating their own learning and development. Any feedback that we give in a self-esteem group therefore needs to be carefully structured. Genuine, meaningful praise and appreciation is just as important for adolescents and adults with low self-esteem as it is for young children, invariably leading to the recipient feeling that what they do and say is valued and of importance. This may seem an obvious point and yet it can prove difficult both to convey this genuineness, and for people with low self-esteem to truly take it on board. Of course, a *formula* for praise and recognition of another person's worth is counter-productive, so the following ideas are simply offered as starting points. Some of these will evidently be most useful for young adolescents since older adolescents and adults may mistakenly see them as patronizing.

- A clear demonstration that we value each person as a unique individual can be conveyed in the simplest of ways, for example by making sure that each person in the group has been acknowledged by name as they arrive, and by giving some indication of pleasure that they are there such as a smile or a 'thumbs up' gesture.

- Use genuine specific, descriptive praise whenever possible:

    'You picked up on Melony's dilemma really quickly in that activity. I liked the way that you adapted the exercise to be more personally relevant for her.'

    'Your pacing was great when you facilitated the group. You gave just enough time to each part of the activity.' (Don't be tempted to add a qualification such as 'You wouldn't have been able to do that a few weeks ago.')

- Give feedback that confirms the personal relevance of current goals:

    'I noticed that you used your goal of pausing and relaxing your shoulders before speaking just then. I got the impression that you were very much in control of what you were saying.'

- Encourage individuals to reflect on what happens during certain chosen activities and during daily routines, picking up on the encounters and strategies that are working well and any moments of difficulty which have been successfully negotiated:

    'You identified very useful ways of giving constructive feedback to someone else. Is there a particular situation where you would be able to use these ideas? Could you tell us how it went next week?'

    See also information sheet 1B, page 72.

- Encourage individuals to give descriptive praise to others. See also the facilitator's notes in Part II, Section 12 regarding appreciations.

- Encourage descriptive self-praise:

    'I asked a really good question in class today. I didn't plan it beforehand and I felt very calm when I spoke.'

    'I talked to someone new and it was hard but I felt good afterwards.'

- Christine Durham, in her book Chasing Ideas (Durham 2006) describes a useful way to make praise a fun interaction for young adolescents. She suggests the use of acronyms and abbreviations such as VIP (very important proposition) or IT (insightful thinking). This could be an ice-breaker activity — perhaps taking familiar acronyms and familiar sayings and encouraging group members to make their own praise messages. For example VIP could be 'Very Imaginative Problem-Solver' or ACE could be 'A Cool Example'. Giving someone a 'thumbs up' sign and saying 'ACE' then becomes even more meaningful.

- Use memory aids if necessary to help you to remember ideas that group members have come up with during some of the activities in this book. Comment on these at a later time to show that you have really thought about what was said. Non-judgemental comments on past experiences and actions can be extremely motivating and self-affirming.

Another useful assumption to make is that each person will *already* be doing something, however small, that is moving them towards their preferred future. Again our task as facilitator is to help individuals to identify exactly what it is that they are already doing. There are several activities throughout Section II which will help with this process.

Motivation

Motivation is difficult to measure. Nonetheless we might instinctively know what it means to *feel* motivated and how much more exciting life is when we are motivated to learn new skills and develop our knowledge. We can support and encourage self-motivation in others by ensuring that activities are intrinsically rewarding (they lead to a tangible change in self-belief, e.g. through the experience of mastering a skill) and extrinsically rewarding (e.g. individuals notice a difference from others in response to their achievements). Such rewards should outweigh the costs in terms of effort. Activities also need to be appropriate for the age and stage of the person and build upon current knowledge and abilities so that possible stresses about absorbing new information and trying out new ideas are minimized and motivation is not inhibited by evaluation apprehension (fear of negative evaluation or ridicule by others).

A person-centred approach to learning

There has been considerable research in education concerning how we learn and how we assimilate our knowledge into daily living. This has resulted in the proposal of several different theories and models. But, despite this increase in available information, there are a few principles that remain relevant. These ideas relate to a set of hypotheses formulated by Carl Rogers in the 1960s, based on his person-centred approach to helping others (Rogers

1969). If you think about your own learning process – what works for you, what doesn't work for you and why this might be – the points outlined below may simply confirm what you already know! They are offered here as a reminder, and within the specific context of supporting the transfer and maintenance of learning related to self-esteem:

Significant learning is more likely to take place when the subject matter is perceived as being personally relevant. 'Perception' is a key concept here. What I, or what others, may think of as being relevant for someone's learning may not be what he *perceives* to be relevant at this point in his life. The timing of feedback (i.e. as soon as possible) and the relative immediacy of being able to use the knowledge and skills in other situations will reinforce the relevance of activities (see earlier section on encouraging self-help, pages 35–37).

It is also important to encourage individuals constantly to ask themselves the question 'Is this relevant to my life?' and '*How* is this relevant to me?'

Learning that involves a change in self-perception may be threatening and can be resisted. This links with Kelly's constructs of transition (see Chapter 2) and is evidently a fairly vital aspect of a self-esteem course! We need to talk about this as being a natural part of the change process for some people and offer practical strategies for moving through resistances when the person is ready to do so (see the Section 5 activity and information sheets 'The Challenge of Change' (on pages 129–43).

Learning that could involve a threat to the self is more easily assimilated when external pressures are at a minimum. Our role here is to ensure as far as possible that the group is a supporting, understanding environment in which change can take place. It is also important to encourage individuals to make use of existing support networks outside the group and to be active in establishing contact with people who will continue to be supportive of the changes they are making (see information sheet 1B, page 72).

Significant learning often takes place through 'doing'. Discussion and reading really are not enough! Einstein highlighted this difference between 'information' and 'knowledge'. I might have some information about Imagework, for example, but I won't truly know its value to me personally unless I try it out in a variety of situations. Experiencing the Imagework within the group and being able (and willing) to apply the activities outside the group are absolutely vital to an individual's success in making changes. It is important to keep referring to this as you work through the sessions together. Participants need to identify how, when and where they can use what they are learning.

Learning is enhanced when we take a responsible role in our own learning process. It may be that some course participants had experience of a very different way of learning in the past. They may have memories of 'being taught' a subject with little or no active participation on their part. A more interactive group may be particularly difficult for them to adjust to. It can also be quite painful for some people to be reflective and proactive in their learning. It requires taking responsibility for oneself and this can feel very frightening, particularly if you have low self-esteem. The 'check-in' groups (see pages 56–57) can help in this process and I strongly recommend that they be incorporated from the start of the course.

Self-initiated learning which involves feelings as well as interest is usually the most lasting and the most comprehensive. We all know that when something suddenly 'grabs our interest' and 'fires our enthusiasm' we are usually much more willing to spend time and energy exploring it. We also know that experiences which help us to change the way we feel about ourselves and the world can leave a lasting impression. Imagework is particularly effective in helping people to connect thoughts, feelings and actions in a safe way. Once again, an atmosphere of openness within a group or when working with an individual can encourage personal insights. This will naturally aid the process of change and the enthusiasm for continued use of those strategies that have worked within structured sessions.

Independence, creativity and self-reliance are supported when self-evaluation is primary and evaluation by others is secondary. The whole structure of a self-esteem course should revolve around this principle. As already mentioned before, we are aiming to encourage realistic self-evaluation through the activities undertaken and through our facilitation – giving accurate 'commentary' on what individuals are doing and then gradually lessening this commentary and encouraging individuals to take over that task for themselves.

It is also important to be aware of how the experience of being in a group can contribute to increasing or decreasing feelings of self-efficacy (see Chapter 1, page 13). Some of the fears that participants may be facing in even the simplest of activities include worries about personal outcome (Will I fail?); evaluation apprehension (What will others think of me? Will I embarrass myself?); feelings of low general efficacy (Will this help?); and low self-efficacy (Will I feel useless?).

The most useful learning involves understanding the learning process and being open to experience. If participants understand how we generally learn and assimilate new ideas and they understand the reasons for doing each of the activities they are much more likely to be able to take their learning into everyday situations (see activity sheet 1.6). Once an individual understands the principles they will be able to modify activities for their own needs. The structure provided by having a general theme throughout the sessions presented in Part II, together with repeated patterns of imagery, will help participants to establish a familiar format for problem-solving and goal-setting, which they can then be guided to use in a variety of situations. In this way individuals can be encouraged in the development of their imaginative and creative skills to support the changes they are making in all areas of their lives.

Summary

In summary, a person is most likely to be able to maintain progress if she:

- is aware of what she is already doing to reach her desired future

- believes that what she is aiming for is personally relevant, achievable and beneficial to herself

- knows from the start what might make things difficult

- has support and encouragement from others

- sets her own realistic yet challenging goals and takes one small step at a time

- takes an active part in finding her own solutions to difficulties

- takes time to recognize and reap the benefits of the goals she has already achieved (enjoys the process!)

- is able to reflect on her successes and failures and realistically self-evaluate (i.e. does not always rely on others to evaluate her progress)

- recognizes 'failures' as being a form of feedback – an indication of how to modify her actions or thoughts

- understands the processes and steps that have led to each success and is able to generalize these to other situations.

Suggestions for further reading

Rogers, C. (1969) *Freedom to Learn: A View of What Education Might Become*. Columbus, OH: Merrill. (See Chapters 7 and 8.)

Working with Groups

This chapter explores some of the principles and practices of group work. I have included it primarily for anyone who is starting to run groups for the first time. Further ideas can be found in the introductory section to Part II.

I remember the group sessions that I ran as a therapist before I had any training as a group facilitator. I muddled through, based on my experiences as a co-worker in other groups, but was more than glad to have some specific guidance from a group counsellor at a later date. These then are just a few basics. Do try to find opportunities for observing or for helping in groups before setting up your own if you can possibly manage it.

Why work on self-esteem in a group setting? There are many advantages to this approach. Groups offer the opportunity for:

- 'on the spot' peer support which could be extended beyond the life of the group

- pooling resources and ideas

- learning and building on social skills

- reducing the facilitator's 'teacher'/'magician' status

- encouraging self-help

- active experimentation to try out new ways of 'being'

- active engagement in the learning process

- spontaneity and creativity as participants try out ideas with more than one person

- encouraging tolerance and respect of other people's ideas

- experiencing positive interaction with peers

- taking the focus away from individuals (but we need to be more aware of individuals not taking full part).

There are also some challenges inherent in this type of group work:

- Groups take a lot of organizing in the early stages. You will need a variety of activities and materials to allow for a variety of learning preferences.

- You need to be aware of how groups function and that you will be encouraging 'group-esteem' as well as individual self-esteem.

- It may take some members a long time to 'find their feet' in a group.

- It may be more tempting to give advice or take over the group during group discussions than if you were working with someone one to one.

- This may be the only social contact that some group members experience and they may unwittingly sabotage their own progress in order to have continued support from the group.

Organizing a group

There are a few issues that need to be addressed with any group. Whatever you decide about these, be clear about the reasons for your decisions and be ready to evaluate the group and review your policies for the next time around. I have, through circumstances rather than informed choice, been faced with all sorts of combinations of group participants. Sometimes, combinations that I originally thought might not work well (e.g. because of differences in age or, in one case, having only one woman in the group and six men) have made for a very cohesive and supportive group because of the personalities of the people involved. Having said this, in general it is best not to have one member who, due to age difference for example, is in danger of feeling isolated because they feel they have little in common with the rest of the group. These then are the main questions you might want to consider:

- Should ages be matched?

- Should the group be single or mixed sex?

- How many is a good number? (I usually work with groups of six to eight.)

- Should the group be closed or open to newcomers once it has started?

Structuring the emotional environment: promoting a person-centred approach

There is certainly no prescriptive formula for the most nurturing personal development group, therapy group or classroom. However, the principles outlined by Carl Rogers (1961) are widely accepted as being an important aspect of effective support. Rogers, the originator of 'person-centred' therapy, believed that each of us has a natural tendency to strive to achieve our full potential in life and he proposed that there are certain conditions which will promote this tendency. These became known as the 'core conditions' for a successful therapeutic alliance but Rogers also made it clear that he felt such conditions were valid for all human relationships. He believed that if he maintained a relationship characterized on his part by congruence ('a genuineness and transparency, in which I am my real feelings'), unconditional positive regard ('warm acceptance of and prizing of the other person as a separate individual') and empathy ('a sensitive ability to see his world and himself as he sees them') then the other person in the relationship would be more self-directing and self-confident and able to cope with life's problems 'more comfortably' (Rogers 1961, pages 37–8). With these principles in mind, the remainder of this chapter explores ways in which we can structure a self-esteem course to maximize feelings of wellbeing and safety for all group members and support them in their journey.

Roles and boundaries

As facilitator, you have responsibility for setting the initial mood or atmosphere of the group experience. New groups can be a scary experience and we need to spend time building trust amongst group members. Trust is most easily established if roles and boundaries are clearly established at the start of a group. This can help participants to feel 'contained' and safe.

Because of the multi-faceted nature of groups there will be multiple roles for those who choose to co-ordinate them. It is important to decide which roles you are taking on at different times and to make it clear to the group that this is what you are doing. However much you may intend for this to be a collaborative group, the initial sessions will undoubtedly involve a greater degree of input from you than later on in the course. This needs to be handled sensitively to discourage or pre-empt any teacher/student expectations that group members may have. Possible roles might include several of the following at any one time:

- role model
- provider of challenges

- facilitator/encourager/enabler

- supporter/helper

- observer

- participant

- researcher/information gatherer/assessor

- provider of fun

- ideas person

- time keeper.

Consider whether or not the roles you are taking on conflict in any way and if so, which one you need to concentrate on. Perhaps a second person is needed to take a different perspective or role? For example, can you be facilitator/encourager and also record information about how individuals are coping with different aspects of a particular activity?

What about the roles of the group members? These too may change and evolve over time so that each person has the opportunity to be the facilitator for a specific activity, or the 'ideas' person, or an observer. Some roles may feel more natural or more scary for individuals. No role should ever be 'forced' on anyone, however well-meaning the intention (e.g. 'Each of you will have had the chance to facilitate a group activity by the end of the course!').

Do not underestimate or devalue your own abilities. Be honest about what you do and don't know and offer your knowledge as a 'resource' for the group. Be willing for some problems to be unresolved. It is not your role to try to make everything better! Occasional self-disclosure of feelings and thoughts can be helpful but should not be too frequent. Allow participants to 'discover' things for themselves.

With regard to boundaries, it is useful to make time limits very clear (e.g. the group will start and finish on time). If someone comes up with something important right at the end of a session do acknowledge the importance but be clear that you are not able to discuss it at that point. For example: 'This is a big issue and it deserves a lot of time, not just the few minutes we can give it now. Let's be sure to talk about it next time.' You might also check with the person to see if there is someone else they can talk it over with before the next meeting.

It is also important to establish group guidelines regarding confidentiality, pre-empting any tendency for discussions about group processes and other members outside the group setting (see Part II, Section 1: 'Getting Started').

Be clear about your own boundaries in terms of the support and time that you are able to give to the group and to individual members.

Reflection

The importance of being reflective lies in the way that we use this skill to develop the most effective way of facilitating change in ourselves and in others. In the context of the activities in this book we certainly need to be aware of our own feelings and needs and the way in which what we do and say has a direct effect on group members.

Larger groups will undoubtedly benefit from having at least two facilitators. It is very difficult to 'hold' a group and to be aware of everything that is going on within and between all the group members if you are working on your own. Having two facilitators gives you the chance to share ideas, keep better track of what is happening and obviously share the responsibility for planning, carrying out and evaluating the sessions. It is also important for each facilitator to be able to reflect on his or her skills as a group leader and to be able to debrief at the end of each session. This is much harder if you are only able to do this infrequently with a peer or at a scheduled supervision session.

Taking time to reflect on the group process and on the session can enable facilitators to deal with the challenges and joys of a group more effectively and to monitor facilitation skills in ways that are most likely to support the group members. An added bonus of course is that constructive discussions with a co-facilitator can help to strengthen personal feelings of competency and self-worth. Box 5.1 highlights questions that you may find useful when planning and reviewing sessions. Don't be put off by the length of the list! Once you have started to run self-esteem groups, you might find it helpful to consider gradually incorporating a few of these over time.

Box 5.1 Questions to aid personal reflection

Starting off

Be clear in your own mind about roles, aims and processes.

Roles

What is my role as facilitator?

How will I set the tone of the sessions/introduce the activities?

Aims

Why are we doing these particular activities? What are my aims/intended outcomes?

How will I know if I have achieved my aims for the group?

Process

What are my personal feelings about these activities? If I was part of this group, would I enjoy doing this?

Are the activities appropriate for the age, developmental level, and cultural backgrounds of the group members?

Who (if anyone) in the group will find the activities difficult/challenging/easy?

Do I need to adapt the activities in any way to allow/encourage full participation of all group members?

What back-up strategies will I need?

How will I handle behaviour that is potentially disruptive to the group?

Am I aware of why this behaviour might occur?

If the group is large or diverse in needs do I have a 'support' person available?

After completion of a session

What went well?

Was there anything that was difficult to monitor?

What skills did I use?

What did I enjoy about the activities?

What did the group members enjoy or find challenging?

Was each activity of an appropriate length?

Was the level right for the whole group?

Did I remember to introduce and summarize activities?

Did I achieve my aims?

Did the group members achieve the intended objectives?

If I were to do a similar session again would I change it in any way? Why?

How would I extend/alter each activity to move the group on to the next stage when they are ready?

Were there any issues raised concerning age, cultural or gender differences which will need to be addressed?

The physical environment

Ensuring physically comfortable and pleasant surroundings for meetings is a sign of how much value we place on the group, how much we respect the group members and how much we respect ourselves as facilitators. This may mean arriving at the venue early enough to switch the heating on and arrange the room before anyone else arrives. It may mean allowing yourself enough time to have a few quiet moments of reflection on your own before the session starts.

Layout

It is important to have a relaxed, informal setting for groups. One of the best ways for this is for the facilitator to set up a circle of comfortable chairs before group members arrive. Remove extra chairs when you know for sure that someone isn't coming to the session but don't remove chairs if you think someone is just going to be late. It is very difficult to join a group session that has already started and doubly difficult if you have low self-esteem. It is also obviously very disruptive to have to ask the whole group to shuffle round in order to fit in an extra chair. Tell the group right at the beginning that the empty chair is for X who you believe will be joining the group a little later this time. Be overt in welcoming that person into the circle when they arrive. When you feel it is appropriate encourage them to contribute something so that they hear their own voice and are acknowledged by the others. A circle enables everyone to keep eye contact when appropriate and allows individual members of the group to take part more easily.

Breaks

If you are going to have a scheduled break make it very clear during the first session how long you are suggesting these breaks should be. This can become a real bone of contention amongst group members if some are keen to restart on time and others amble back ten minutes later. However, it may be that group members need the chance to talk informally during a slightly longer break than you had originally planned. If an activity has been particularly challenging just before a break then participants may need extra time to relax afterwards. Late returners may be indicating something about how

Helping group members to be reflective thinkers is also a vital part of the process. Activities that allow members the opportunity to 'pause and reflect' in a constructive way can greatly aid the emergence of appropriate strategies and can result in insights which may otherwise be missed.

they are feeling! You might want to involve the group in negotiating timings after the first session. This will also introduce the idea of participants having more say in how the group evolves. Breaks are not just 'added extras', they can in fact be a very valuable part of the session.

Warm ups

New groups require time spent in getting to know each other. It is important to build up your own repertoire of group 'warm up' activities to help participants to feel relaxed about sharing their thoughts and ideas. I have a personal aversion to 'gelling' games for adults – I have had to endure them in too many groups that I have attended as a participant – and so my personal preference is for simpler 'getting to know you' activities in pairs and threes to start with. I have, however, included two slightly more active questionnaire exercises in the activity sheets in recognition of the fact that not everyone will feel like me about such activities!

Using appropriate role models and peer facilitators

People often learn best from others who have been through similar circumstances and have 'come through'. Time and again, when asked to identify the single most useful aspect of working in a group, clients have reported the benefit of being with others 'just like me'. They have also referred to the usefulness of hearing how others have dealt successfully with difficult situations and have made progress throughout the life of the group. In many instances clients have reported being motivated by the successes of others and by the support that individual group members can offer to each other in the setting of goals and the realistic monitoring of successes and difficulties.

Group facilitators should seriously consider the possibility of inviting previous group members to come and talk to new groups but this needs to be timely in order for the group to feel motivated and supported in their own struggles – too early and it could lead to demotivation, too late and the impact will be lessened.

The life of a group – the beginning phase

Groups hold all sorts of different associations for people and this aspect needs to be recognized and explored as early as possible. Coming to a group may initially heighten feelings of inadequacy; being different, depending on others (I can't cope on my own) and so on. Perhaps some participants arrive wanting or even demanding a quick 'cure' and feel disheartened when they discover that change of this nature is going to take time and commitment. Others arrive full of hope and ready to take a leap of faith into unknown territory, possibly without any safety net! A primary task in this phase of the course is therefore helping group members to get to grips with the whole idea of being in a group and of 'finding their place' (see Section 1 activity sheets 1–6).

Middles and ends

By the time the group sessions are halfway through you will probably have found that people are beginning to regroup and form different bonds. They are beginning to 'find' their role in the group. Sometimes this role can be gently challenged so that people can experiment with change. For example, someone who always agrees with whatever anyone else says can be encouraged to go first in a round and to put forward their own idea before anyone else.

For some group members, ending the group will be a natural stage and will not cause any undue concerns. For others, the ending of a group may feel like a great loss and what they experience may reflect how they generally deal with endings in life. You will need to prepare for the ending of the group well in advance. I suggest that you might start to mention it at least two weeks before the final session. Talk about what will happen next; about self-help and continuing to set goals; about saying goodbye to each other and about how they can capitalize on what they have learnt. There may be some disappointments about what has not been achieved as well as recognition of successes and these also need to be voiced and acknowledged. Although all these things will have been discussed throughout the course it is useful to bring all the 'threads' together in the final few weeks.

You may feel that it would be useful for groups to meet up again for a follow-up a few weeks after the course has finished. This can be very beneficial in that people have the chance to catch up on what has been happening with each other and to talk about their successes. They can perhaps support each other in problem-solving something specific that they would like to work on. However, be aware that regular follow-ups run by the same facilitator each time could encourage dependency rather than self-help.

Make sure that there is opportunity for a celebration in the last session. This could so easily be missed out because of lack of time or because it is not given due importance. It is, however, very important to complete the group in this way. It defines the end of the life of the group as it stands. It gives weight to acknowledging everyone's achievements and it shows that enjoyment and celebration are part of building self-esteem.

Suggestions for further reading

Dwivedi, K.N. (ed.) (1999) *Group Work with Children and Adolescents: A Handbook.* London: Jessica Kingsley Publishers.

Ernst, S. and Goodison, L. (1992) *In Our Own Hands: A Book of Self-Help Therapy.* London: The Women's Press.

Houston, G. (1990) *The Red Book of Groups.* London: The Rochester Foundation.

Jacobs, M. (1992) *Swift to Hear: Facilitating Skills in Listening and Responding.* London: SPCK.

Summary

The approach to building self-esteem that I have proposed in these introductory chapters is constantly evolving in response to my own learning and experiences and in response to discussions with others. Yet, despite the organic nature of this model, there are certain underlying principles which have endured:

- Self-esteem has its roots in our earliest interactions as babies. It is a complex aspect of our lives. Enhancing self-esteem is therefore a multi-layered undertaking.

- Supporting someone in building and maintaining healthy self-esteem ultimately involves a way of being rather than a procedure with an end product, or something we do to make people 'feel better'.

- When we engage with others in building and maintaining healthy self-esteem we should do so with mindfulness, integrity and respect for each person's unique journey.

- When we are able to be in tune with another person's concerns and dilemmas, through our own mindfulness, then we have greater potential to strengthen rapport, build trust and increase the possibility for long-lasting change.

Part II

Activities with Guidelines

Introduction

Using the information sheets

As already noted in the Introduction to Part I, the information sheets can be used in individual work with clients and pupils as well as with groups. These can also be adapted for discussion rather than used as handouts if needed. I have suggested further reading for some of these sheets, but this is not essential to being able to lead the discussions.

Using the activity sheets

After Section 1, 'Getting Started', each activity section links with the eight foundation elements for self-esteem/wellbeing (see Chapter 1, 'Self-Esteem and Wellbeing') and each of the summary sheets that conclude Sections 2 to 12 links with the following section to give a logical flow to the different areas covered. Most of the activities are self-explanatory, and many could, therefore, also be used for 'do at home' exercises if you feel this is appropriate. Of course, anything that seems too much like 'homework' may well be resisted but wherever possible, I would encourage a gradual increase in the amount that participants undertake outside the group. They could also be encouraged to do their own research on different topics (see Chapter 4, 'Learning and Generalizing Knowledge and Skills' and Chapter 5, 'Working with Groups').

I have found it helpful to have a few prompt questions prepared to ease the discussion for both the information sheets and for the activities but would always recommend encouragement of the group members' initial personal reflections. The facilitator is responsible for demonstrating and encouraging the respect and acceptance that group members may be lacking elsewhere in their lives (externally and/or internally). Unconditional acceptance and genuine constructive feedback in response to insights from group members will help to promote confidence and motivation. Having said this, it is important to try to discourage lengthy problem-focused discussions and any re-telling of 'how things have always gone wrong'. Acknowledge the difficulties experienced and steer the group towards a solution-focused approach.

Examples of prompt questions

What are your first thoughts about this topic? How do you feel after doing this activity?

How could this activity help you to…?

Was it easy or difficult to complete this activity? Why was that?

Did you discover anything that surprised you?

Is there anything from this activity/topic that you would want to share with a friend? Who else do you think you could talk with about this?

Look for opportunities to allow more reticent members to speak but avoid putting anyone 'on the spot' to answer a question.

General guidelines for facilitating imagery exercises

The imagery exercises presented in Part II of this book are mostly adapted from more in-depth Imagework formulated by Dina Glouberman (e.g. Glouberman 2003, 2010) or they have 'emerged' while I have been facilitating group sessions. Some are the result of combining exercises from Imagework and Neurolinguistic Programming (NLP); Imagework and Personal Construct Theory (see Part I, Chapter 2); or Imagework and Solution Focused Brief Therapy (e.g. Berg and de Shazer 1993). You do not need specific training in any of these fields in order to lead the Imagework activities. If you are familiar with a different approach to supporting change I believe that you will find Imagework an adaptable tool that can be used to complement your own training.

Where there are a series of dots in the Imagework exercises this indicates that you will need to give plenty of time to allow participants to explore an image. Keep your voice as calm as possible both for the Imagework sections and when you are doing the relaxation exercises.

Imagery exercises lend themselves to being highly interactive. As a facilitator, you will find it useful if participants give you an indication of what is happening with their images as they work with them. This will help you to pace your instructions and allows time to those who need to explore images more deeply, or who are having difficulty getting an image in the first place. Verbal feedback of this kind also fosters feelings of connectedness between group members, who may sometimes be working with their eyes closed in order to concentrate on their images. Once again, I have suggested relevant questions that you might ask in conjunction with each imagery activity.

When you are waiting for participants to produce their own images in a group, ask them to raise a finger rather than calling out to indicate that they have thought of one. This avoids disrupting others who have not yet 'found' their image.

Invariably the group will not all be working at the same pace. Move on when it feels right to do so.

Most people are able to access images quite easily in one-to-one sessions but some may find it harder in a group, especially if they feel there is a 'right' way of getting an image. You will need to assure everyone at the outset that whatever images emerge for them are OK. If someone indicates that they are having difficulty you can help them by using any or all of the following suggestions:

- There is plenty of time. As you watch, just let the image come to you.

- Don't worry if the image is a bit hazy to start with. It will gradually become clearer as you work with it.

- Imagine that the nothingness that you can see is a dark curtain. As you draw the curtain aside notice what image emerges.

- If you *could* see an image, what would it be?!

- Don't worry if you are having difficulty seeing the image clearly; just get a sense of what it might be and work with that.

On completion of an Imagework activity the process is often recorded through drawing, movement, poetry or story. This can be an incredibly powerful way of holding the Imagework experience in mind: 'Once we have entertained an image, it is always potentially present to our gaze.... This is the basis of art therapy or journal-keeping: making a home for certain images that have been transforming' (Moore 1992, pages 64–5). I suggest that you always have a ready supply of paper (preferably of different colours) and pencils, crayons, pastels and so on. Even a brief sketch or a few key words will suffice, although generally I have found that participants like to spend quite a long time recording their Imagework in this way.

Using 'check-in groups' and closing circles

During the early sessions in particular you may find that a few people have been very verbal or have taken up a large proportion of the allocated time because they were working on a particular issue in more depth.

One way of ensuring that everyone feels 'heard' and part of the group is to ask everyone to check in with how they are feeling at the start and then have a closing circle where everyone says one thing before they leave.

Checking in

Where there are six or more participants it is better to facilitate the 'check-in' times by splitting into smaller groups of three or four. The full format for these groups is outlined below and I have experienced the power of this in a variety of groups with mixed ages and sexes. I do, however, use an adapted form at times if I think the group would find it too difficult to sit with eyes closed or to sit silently between speakers at this early stage of the course.

Sit in a close circle and make contact of some sort (e.g. one hand on the arm of the chairs either side of you or feet just touching). Close eyes. Relax. Tune into yourself. Notice what your body is feeling. Notice where your thoughts are drifting to. Be aware of the other people in the small group then tune back into yourself again. The first person to speak takes one minute (this can be extended as the weeks progress) to talk about how they are feeling or anything else that comes to mind at that moment. The other members of the group simply listen. The speaker is told when their one minute is coming to an end. As facilitator you could say something such as 'start to draw that to a close now' or 'just finishing what you are saying…'. The speaker then sits quietly for a few moments while the listeners silently 'send' their complete acceptance. The speaker is asked to be open to receive this acceptance. This may seem a difficult concept for some at first but explain that there is no right or wrong way of doing this. Group members do not talk between speakers. After a few moments ask everyone to tune back into themselves and then the next person in the circle has their chance to speak. Repeat the process for each person in the group. When everyone has had their turn they can open their eyes and spend five minutes giving each other any feedback as appropriate. The feedback must of course be non-judgemental. It could be something like: 'I really felt for you when you said…'; 'I think I know how you feel when…'; 'You sounded excited when you talked about…'.

So for these check-in groups to work well you need to establish the format beforehand with the group:

- Explain that they will have their eyes closed so that, as speakers, they can concentrate on what they are feeling and on what they want to say rather than thinking about any feedback they might or might not get from the others in the group. As listeners, they can focus on listening to what is being said.

- Explain that it is fine if they don't feel like talking for the whole time allotted but that their turn will still be the same length as everyone else's.

- Explain about 'sending' and 'receiving' acceptance.

- Explain the type of feedback that is acceptable for the end of the check-in period.

Throughout the course you can gradually increase the time for each person to speak when this feels right but the maximum time should be five minutes (three minutes is usually ample). Ideally you should have equal numbers in each mini circle. Keep an eye on the time and don't be tempted to give some people longer than others. After the first few times of doing this you could begin to use this time for people to check in with how they feel about a given topic. For example, everyone says whatever comes to mind on the topic of confidence or relationships or anger.

I first came across this format when I was doing my Imagework training. Dina Glouberman refers to this as 'Oekos groups' from the Greek word for home. It is an amazingly effective way of ensuring that everyone has their turn and that everyone feels that they have been listened to and accepted for who they are.

Closing circles

At the end of each meeting bring everyone back together again in a circle and finish with each person having the chance to say one brief thing before they leave. This closing circle can be more structured than the check-in groups. I usually offer an idea for people to complete in their own words. For example:

I feel…

Today I found out that…

Today I felt…

My name is _____ and I am…

I have noticed that…

I feel really good about…

My next step is…

I want to say that…

Today this group has given me…

Section 1

Getting Started

Aims of this section

- to give an overview of the course content

- to introduce the concept of self-help

- to begin to establish group identity and cohesion

Information and activity sheets

INFORMATION SHEET 1A: INTRODUCTION (PAGE 65)

This information sheet can be given to participants prior to the start of the course and/or used as a basis for group discussion during the first session. It is important to establish the idea that the course is based on self-help and that the aim is to assist each member of the group to find their own way to build self-esteem successfully.

You will need to be familiar with the basic concepts underpinning the use of imagery and personal construct theory (see Part I, Chapters 2 and 3) in order to be able to explain these points more fully if questioned. However, this is also a good opportunity to establish the idea that opinions and suggestions are welcomed from all group members and that, once they know each other a little better, participants may want to say what they understand by each of the points on subsequent information sheets. Help individuals to clarify their own reasons for being in the group. Be aware that there may be conflicting aims or misunderstandings about the purpose of the group and these will need to be addressed from the outset.

Suggested reading
Jacobs, M. (1992) *Swift to Hear: Facilitating Skills in Listening and Responding.* London: SPCK.

1.1 GETTING TO KNOW THE GROUP (PAGE 66)

This is one way of getting people moving around and speaking to others in a relaxed way. Set a time limit (maximum of ten minutes) according to the size of the group.

An alternative way of doing this is to have a collection of cards on which there are single words or pictures of things people might like to do or like to eat. For example, your list might include such things as watching soap operas, chocolate, cycling, singing, dogs, football, burgers and so on. Try to include some things that you think only one or two people might like. Distribute the cards evenly around the group. Each person has to get rid of their cards by asking the question 'Do you like _____?' and handing over the appropriate card if the other person says 'Yes'. At the same time they have to find out as many names as possible. The aim is to have as few cards as you can by the end of the time limit. This does, of course, require honesty in saying if you like something or not!

1.2 REMEMBERING NAMES (PAGE 67)

This could also be done by asking everyone to come up with a way that they would like to be described, using adjectives beginning with the first letter of their name, for example cool Cathy, stylish Steve, relaxed Rajeev. Or you could introduce the use of imagery at this stage by suggesting that participants think of an image that they associate with each person in the group. This could be literal, e.g. Rajeev relaxing in an armchair, or metaphorical, e.g. Rajeev as a sleeping cat. These images may well change as the course progresses and members come to know each other in more depth.

For a longer exercise, invite participants to share the story of their name, what they know of its origin, how it was chosen, etc. This could be done in pairs or in the whole group if time allows.

1.3 BEING PART OF A GROUP (PAGE 68)

This is to be completed individually and then discussed in pairs. Ask for group contributions to the last section: 'What would help me to feel most comfortable in this group?' This could form the basis for establishing the group guidelines to help foster the feeling of trust amongst those taking part and to help ensure that the group is a safe place to be. Help members to establish guidelines for the 'life' of the group and offer periodic reminders if necessary. Such guidelines might include the following:

- Respect other people and their contributions to the group. Avoid judging or criticizing.

- The group will start and finish on time.

- No alcohol/drugs to be brought into the group.

- Anything said within the group is confidential and cannot be shared with non-group members unless there are issues of safety involved.

See also activity sheet 1.4, 'Communication guidelines'.

Feeling part of a group and being accepted and appreciated by a group gives us a sense of belonging and helps us to feel good about ourselves, especially when our internal reserves are low. Sometimes, however, we may find ourselves behaving in ways that don't truly reflect our self-concept in order to *appear* to fit in with a group. Young adolescents can be particularly vulnerable to this sort of peer pressure. They may try to 'fit in' with a group because they think they ought to or because it's 'cool' or exciting. There may be times when this is OK and also times when it's not OK, when trying to fit in leads to them feeling awkward or unhappy. It is important to acknowledge this natural wish to feel accepted and liked and to explore successful ways of achieving this. There is scope for this to be revisited throughout the course if needed.

1.4 COMMUNICATION GUIDELINES (PAGE 69)

These can be usefully incorporated into the general group 'guidelines' and revisited periodically to encourage group members to continue to use them. It is important for participants to understand the relevance of each point and the possible effects on self-esteem when these guidelines are forgotten.

Listening accurately. There are specific activities for this later in the course (activity sheet 9.5). At this stage, participants can be encouraged to listen to each other fully and to try not to make assumptions about what someone else might be thinking. Talk about how a person's own anxieties may get in the way of listening accurately to someone else.

Using 'I' not 'you'. This is often a difficult task for new groups, but is a helpful pattern to establish from the outset. Saying something like 'You know what it's like in groups, you don't want to speak up because you feel embarrassed' may reflect what the speaker feels but is unable to voice directly. Such statements also encourage assumptions about what people feel generally in groups. If the speaker is able to say 'I don't want to speak up because I feel embarrassed', this allows much greater possibility for personal change. Another useful idea to introduce at this point is the way that we sometimes appear to hand over responsibility for how we feel to others. A statement such as 'You make me angry' assumes a very different locus of control in comparison to 'I feel angry about what you just said'.

Giving constructive feedback. This will also be revisited when the group talk about assertiveness skills (activity sheets 7.9 and 7.10). At this point group members can be encouraged to make their feedback to others positive and precise (see also guidelines for 'check-in' groups, pages 56–57).

Avoiding labelling. Encourage individuals to remember the often quoted (but worth repeating!) warning to avoid 'labelling' – even if this is just a private thought. For example, instead of someone thinking of herself as 'shy' she could try to be more specific: 'At the moment I am unsure of myself when I first arrive somewhere new. It takes me a while to build the confidence to talk to new people. It might help if I practised some things that I could say.'

Recognizing personal values. This is an obvious point, but worth bringing up for discussion at the start of a group. Participants can be encouraged to reflect on the fact that they may have different guiding principles in life and whilst we might disagree with each other over certain values, it is not the job of the group to challenge these. Individual differences in social customs, beliefs and behaviours should be acknowledged and an atmosphere of open discussion should be encouraged. Group members need to feel safe enough to be able to say what is the accepted 'norm' for their family or culture.

Looking for the common goal. Recognizing that each person is taking part in the course because they have concerns about self-esteem (and reminding participants that this is the case) can help to clear up misunderstandings between group members. For example, on a very basic level, two people working in a pair may have different ideas about how to get something done. Keeping an eye on the fact that they both want a similar outcome may help them to come to a workable solution.

1.5 FEELINGS AND EXPECTATIONS (PAGE 70)

This is to be completed individually and discussed in pairs. Common themes could be shared with the whole group to help members to recognize that they have similar worries or expectations. As a group exercise I also like to collate the 'hopes' for the group and write them on a large sheet of paper inside a drawing of a cooking pot. I then draw in some flames beneath the pot and talk about simmering the contents during the course. This gives me a better understanding of what group members are looking for and can be revisited periodically to check progress and make additions. Of course, like any soup or stew, the sum of the individual ingredients may produce something new and surprising!

1.6 HOW DO YOU LEARN BEST? (PAGE 71)

Ideas for discussions about learning can be found in Part I, Chapter 4, 'Learning and Generalizing Knowledge and Skills'. This brief exercise introduces the idea of taking responsibility for personal outcomes.

INFORMATION SHEET 1B: HOW YOU CAN BENEFIT MOST FROM THIS COURSE (PAGE 72)

This is another reminder to participants that the group is a vehicle for developing self-help strategies (see Part I, Chapter 4).

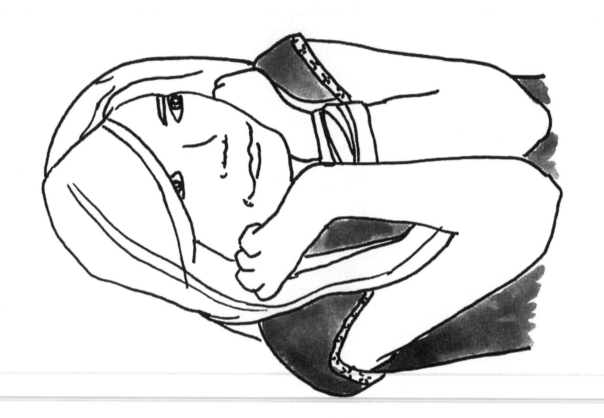

Getting Started

Introduction

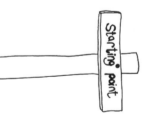

This course has been designed to help you to help yourself. The activity sheets and discussion topics will provide you with the opportunity to explore different aspects of self-esteem and to begin to make the changes that you want.

Here are some important points to keep in mind as you make a start:

- We all have the ability to solve problems and to make effective changes in our lives. Sometimes we need to remind ourselves of how to do this.

- Change of any sort affects us on all levels. For example a change in the way that you think about a certain situation can lead to changes in how you feel physically and in how you behave in that situation.

- Some parts of this course may at first seem more relevant to you than other parts. This is natural. Each of us is a unique individual with differing needs and interests.

- Remember, we are constantly changing throughout our lives. This means that at any stage of life there is always the possibility of developing and maintaining healthy self-esteem.

1.1 Getting to know the group

Find as many people as possible in the group who can agree with the following statements. Write their names in the space provided.

I own a bicycle (and I use it)

I have a pet

I enjoy watching sport

I have seen one of my favourite films more than three times

I like spicy food

It took me more than one hour to get here today

I play a musical instrument

I have an unusual hobby

I don't like chocolate

1.2 Remembering names

Names are an important part of who we are. You may have chosen to shorten your name or use a nickname to reflect how you would like to be known. Remembering other people's names is an important skill too and there are many strategies that can help you to do this. One is to associate the person's name with something else – an object, something they like doing, a colour they like to wear and so on. For each person in the group, note down something that will help you to remember his or her name.

Name	Memory aid

Group Members

1.3 Being part of a group

Throughout life most of us have the chance to be part of many different groups, including family, school, work, sport and friendship groups. You may feel more comfortable in some types of group than others and you will have developed certain ways of 'being' and thinking about yourself in these different groups. It is important to recognize that you have some choice about this.

How I would like to be in this group

What would help me to feel most comfortable in this group?

How I normally cope with groups

What I believe I can contribute to this group

1.4 Communication guidelines

These guidelines are important for all communications and will be useful to keep in mind throughout the course. When you have discussed them in your group, write what you feel each of these guidelines involves.

Listening accurately

Using 'I', not 'you'

Giving constructive feedback

Avoiding labelling

Recognizing personal values

Looking for the common goal

1.5 Feelings and expectations

As you complete each section of this course you will discover that you have a greater degree of control over the way you choose to lead your life and your ability to set and accomplish goals. Take a few moments first to think about where you are starting from.

What are your feelings as you start the course? What do you feel confident about?

What would you like to know more about?

What would you like to have achieved by the end of this course?

What do you think are the main difficulties that you will need to overcome?

1.6 How do you learn best?

Think about your experiences of learning new ideas and skills. What has worked well for you in the past? What has not worked well?

Imagine that it is the end of the course and you feel that it has been a useful experience. As you look back on what happened ask yourself 'What did I do that helped me to enjoy the course?'

How You Can Benefit Most From This Course

Keep referring to the course notes

The activity sheets are designed to be used alongside group sessions and also as a resource for self-help following completion of the course. Use your notes and drawings to remind yourself about the points that seemed most important to you.

Devote specific time to working on your current goals

As well as the time you are involved in the group, it is important that you set aside a short period every day when you are thinking about one particular goal with your full concentration. You will find that as you get used to the different ideas and strategies, they will become a natural part of your daily life. However, spending time on them every day will help you to gain maximum benefit in a shorter time.

Make the course personally relevant

As you go through each activity ask yourself what relevance it has to you and how you can apply it to your own life. Make notes as often as you can when thoughts occur to you and when each area is being discussed in your group. Make a point of acting on ideas straight away while they are still fresh in your mind.

Seek support

Discuss this course and the goals you are setting with as many friends and members of your family as possible. This will help you to remember important ideas and is also a major step forward in building your self-esteem. You will, of course, have the support of the group facilitators and other group members, but as you make more and more changes it will be helpful to have support and encouragement from outside the group too.

Section 2

What Is Self-Esteem?

- to offer some basic information about how self-esteem develops

- to start the exploration of personal self-esteem

- to introduce the use of imagery as a way of exploring personal patterns of thinking and feeling

- to introduce the idea that our thoughts have a direct effect on how we behave and develop

Information and activity sheets

INFORMATION SHEETS 2A: SELF-CONCEPT AND SELF-ESTEEM AND 2B: GLOBAL AND SPECIFIC SELF-ESTEEM (PAGES 80–81)

These information sheets can form the basis for a discussion about the fact that we can build different areas of self-esteem in our lives (instead of thinking of self-esteem only in terms of a global sense of self-worth and competency). For example, a person may feel OK about her ability and her self-worth with regard to forming friendships but not OK about her ability to be an artist. If 'being artistic' is important in her life then any negative comments by others could potentially damage her global sense of self-esteem. This pitfall can be avoided if she is able to realistically self-evaluate, recognize her own strengths and abilities and acknowledge her feelings of self-worth in other areas.

Levels of self-esteem within specific areas might also fluctuate simply because of the type of task that we are undertaking, our mood at the time or the attitude of the important people in our lives. It is important for someone with low self-esteem to recognize the normality of this.

Suggested reading

Harter, S. (1999) *The Construction of the Self.* New York: Guilford Press.
Satir, V. (1991) *Peoplemaking.* London: Souvenir Press.

2.1 BEING SPECIFIC (PAGE 82)

Possible areas might be:

- relationships with friends
- relationships with family
- relationship with partner
- meeting new people
- independence
- work
- school/college
- creative projects.

For each broad area participants then identify one specific aspect. For example under 'independence' a person might identify 'travelling alone'.

2.2 FUTURE ME! (PAGE 83)

This is based on the 'My future self' exercise by Dina Glouberman (2003, pages 186–191).

Each member of the group chooses a specific situation to work with. Guide the whole group through the imagery exercise. If you feel comfortable to do so, I suggest that you familiarize yourself with the instructions beforehand and then use your own wording, as this will sound more natural. (See also 'General guidelines for facilitating imagery exercises' on pages 54–55.) Leave plenty of time between each part of the exercise for everyone to explore their chosen situation in their imagination. Ask for contributions so that the exercise feels interactive rather than static. The exchange might go something like this:

Facilitator: Imagine that it's the end of the situation now and it really didn't go well at all. Ask yourself 'What is the feeling that I have right now?' ... and 'How did I get here?' ... Would anyone like to say the feeling and how you got there?

Group member 1: I rushed and got confused.

Facilitator: OK. So rushing meant that you felt confused.

Group member 2: I wasn't given enough time.

Facilitator: You weren't given enough time and that meant that . . . ?

Group member 2: I felt panicky.

Facilitator: You didn't have enough time so then you felt panicky . . . OK. So now ask yourselves 'What was I thinking just before this situation?'

[and so on].

We don't want to dwell on the negative aspects of a situation, of course. However, this exercise can often bring up some very positive ways of tackling obstacles. The next activity sheet should be completed with only the positive outcome in mind.

The self-fulfilling prophecy is an important concept. For example, someone who expects things to turn out poorly and believes with absolute certainty that he will fail is obviously not setting himself up for success! A positive attitude *accompanied by realistic assessment of abilities will invariably lead to more positive outcomes.*

2.3 EXPECTATIONS (PAGE 84)

Draw together any links that people can come up with between thoughts and actions and the idea of self-fulfilling prophecies.

2.4 WHY IS IT IMPORTANT TO RAISE OUR LEVELS OF SELF-ESTEEM? (PAGE 85)

If it has not already been discussed this would be a good opportunity to talk about having 'healthy' levels of self-esteem rather than necessarily thinking in terms of 'high' levels of self-esteem. 'Healthy' will be wherever the individual feels comfortable with who they are. Healthy self-esteem also involves awareness of others and their needs and feelings. Building self-esteem is not about feeling so good about yourself that you lose sight of where you fit into family and friendship groups and wider society. (See Part 1, Chapter 1, 'Self-Esteem and Wellbeing'.)

Brainstorm the benefits of healthy self-esteem. Some possible benefits are:

- greater enjoyment of life
- increased possibility to develop specific strengths/qualities
- increased ability to deal with difficult situations
- more likely to be able to take worthwhile risks

- increased ability to tolerate own mistakes
- increased ability to cope with changes
- ability to develop secure, fulfilling relationships more easily
- increased ability to develop a greater understanding of other people.

See also Part I, Chapter 1, 'Self-Esteem and Wellbeing'.

2.5 AN IMAGE OF HEALTHY SELF-ESTEEM (PAGE 86)

Lead the whole group in this exercise. As before, ask for contributions every now and then. Leave plenty of pauses for people to come up with images and explore them thoroughly. The last question: 'What advice do I have for self?' encourages people to view themselves from a different perspective. For example, my image of self-esteem at the moment of writing these words is a buttercup (I have had many different images of self-esteem over the course of writing this book, but not a buttercup before!). As the buttercup I want to tell 'self' (Deborah) 'chin up!' and I suddenly remember that this comes from a childhood pursuit of placing a buttercup under your chin to reflect the sunlight! (See also previous guidelines for facilitating imagery exercises, pages 54–55.)

Take time at the end of the exercise to give everyone the chance to talk about their experience of this imagery or to show their drawing. This can be done in pairs or in the whole group.

Remind everyone that we cannot interpret images for each other. Our images have unique meanings and only the 'image-maker' will know their significance. However, talking about a personal image can often help the person to clarify in their own mind what the image means to them.

2.6 PERSONAL CHECKLIST (PAGES 87–88)

The boxes can be shaded to the degree to which each statement is thought to be true. For example, 'Very true' would mean the whole box is shaded, 'Quite true' would mean perhaps just a small part of the box being shaded and 'Not true at all' would obviously mean no shading. The checklist could be revisited at various stages throughout the course to help participants to review their progress. This is also an opportunity for participants to do a 'reality' check, by discussing their list with other group members or with a facilitator. I doubt very much that any of us could confidently shade all the boxes completely at any one moment in our lives. There will always be fluctuations in self-awareness, moments of self-doubt, memories from the past and worries about the future. The checklist is simply an aid to focusing on certain elements of our thinking that can enhance or hinder our continued growth.

The blank box at the end of the checklist can be used as a personal 'bonus' box where individuals can write a positive statement about themselves.

INFORMATION SHEET 2C: THE ICEBERG OF SELF-ESTEEM (PAGE 89)

Facilitate a group discussion about how little or how much we 'reveal' our emotions and thoughts. For some people, some covert aspects of a difficulty may be displayed overtly although not necessarily in a way that might be expected. For example, embarrassment may 'appear' in the form of verbal aggression. See also information sheet 4B and activity sheet 4.2.

2.7 MY PERSONAL ICEBERG OF SELF-ESTEEM (PAGE 90)

Brainstorm this as a whole group. Each person can then select the relevant elements for their own iceberg. This is also another tool for self-help at a later date. As some elements are reduced or eliminated there will be a knock-on effect on others so the iceberg can be redrawn. Participants can then compare the different versions of their own icebergs at different stages of the course. The following is a sample compilation of responses from groups that I have facilitated:

Overt elements:

fidgeting, blushing, looking away, walking away, sweating,

biting fingernails, tearful, tense muscles,

restricted interactions with others, 'tongue-tied'

Covert elements:

feeling 'awkward', embarrassed, 'churned up' inside,

angry, frustrated, depressed, negative self-talk,

lethargic, 'everything is an effort'

Of course, this could also be completed as an iceberg of *healthy* self-esteem to further emphasize the connections between thoughts, feelings and behaviours and how these interact.

2.8 SUMMARY (PAGE 91)

Allocate specific time at the end of a group session for completion of the summary sheet. If it is completed within the group then there is opportunity for group members to ask questions and to seek help in formulating a positive intention if needed. If you feel it is appropriate, you may want to share a favourite quote about intentions. One that appeals to me is from Gary Zukav's book, *The Seat of the Soul:*

Every experience, and every change in your experience, reflects an intention. An intention is not only a desire. It is the use of your will... If you truly desire to change (something) that change begins with the intention to change it. How it will change depends upon the intention that you set. (Zukav 1991, page 106)

Positive intentions need to be precise and stated in the first person. Even though it is an intention it should be written in the present tense as we are making an assumption that some part of it has already started to happen (see Part I, Chapter 4, 'Learning and Generalizing Knowledge and Skills'). Some examples might be:

'I am building my self-esteem'

'I am more open about how I feel in the group'

'I am expressing my opinions in group discussions'

'I am using accurate listening'

What Is Self-Esteem?

Self-Concept and Self-Esteem

Our *self-concept* is the overall view that we have of ourselves, including our appearance, abilities, attitudes and beliefs.

Our self-concept develops over time and is mostly based on the way in which we interpret the reactions we get from other people. This process begins with our earliest interactions as babies.

Generally, we try to act in a way that fits in with our self-concept. When new information is received to add to our system of beliefs about ourselves we may, therefore, use a process of *'filtering'*. This means that if the information fits in with our self-concept we will probably accept it as being true. If it doesn't fit in with how we see ourselves then we might ignore it, misinterpret it or reject it completely.

In this way our beliefs affect how we see the world and this in turn affects what we do and say. Even if we have beliefs about ourselves that don't match with reality they are true for us because we *believe* them to be true.

Self-esteem is about the value we place on ourselves and our abilities. If a person's view of herself (her self-concept) is close to how she would like to be (her 'ideal' self) then she can be said to have healthy self-esteem. An 'ideal' self can be a self who accepts all aspects of her personality and who feels comfortable with who she is. 'Ideal' doesn't have to mean perfect!

We can have different levels of self-esteem in different areas of our lives. These levels can change according to circumstances. For example, self-esteem is often affected when a relationship that was important to us has come to an end.

A person with healthy self-esteem feels OK about being herself while still respecting the needs and feelings of others.

Global and Specific Self-Esteem

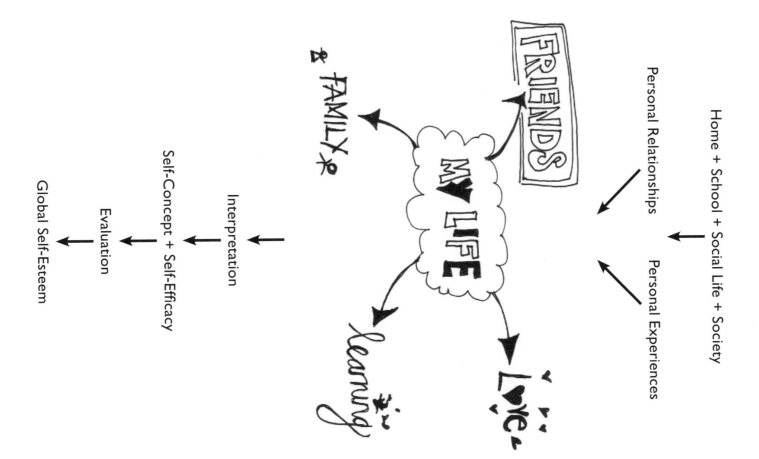

Home + School + Social Life + Society

Personal Relationships

Personal Experiences

FRIENDS

MY LIFE

FAMILY

learning

Love

Interpretation

Self-Concept + Self-Efficacy

Evaluation

Global Self-Esteem

2.1. Being specific

Think of some different areas in your life where you would like to have a greater feeling of self-esteem.

2.2 Future me!

You might find yourself thinking about past mistakes or difficulties and worry about whether or not things will always be like that, or worry that the same thing will happen again. Although we can't change what someone else might do or say in a situation, we can change our own thoughts and actions. In this next exercise you will be able to identify ways in which what you do and what you think influence the outcome of a particular situation. Imagining an event as if it had already happened and imagining both a negative and then a positive outcome in this way can be very powerful.

Look at the previous activity sheet and choose one area of self-esteem that you would like to concentrate on first. Now think of a specific situation which, if tackled successfully, would boost your self-esteem in this area. For example the category you choose might be 'being more independent' and a specific situation might be 'making an official phone call confidently'.

Read through the following instructions or have someone read them to you. When you are ready, close your eyes and relax your body. Imagine that it is the end of the situation you chose. Imagine that things did not go well. Ask yourself the following questions, making sure that you give yourself plenty of time to think about each question in turn:

- What is the feeling that I have right now? How did I get to this feeling?

- What was I thinking before and during the situation?

- What did I say/not say?

- What was I feeling physically before and during the situation?

- What was the main decision or attitude that got me here?

- What else do I notice about what happened?

Now let that image go. Give your body a bit of a shake and then settle back into a relaxed position again. Remember, you are imagining that the event has already happened. This time you are feeling good because things went really well. Ask yourself the following questions:

- Exactly what is the 'good' feeling that I have now? How did I get to this feeling?

- What was I thinking before and during the situation?

- What did I say/not say?

- What was I feeling physically before and during the situation?

- What was the main decision or attitude that got me here?

- What else do I notice about what happened?

Remember in all this to use your 'memory' from the future, not your 'thoughts' about what it might be like.

2.3 Expectations

When you are ready, make notes for yourself about what you imagined. Discuss this with one other person in the group. Did you have any thoughts in common?

The situation I chose was:

What I did, thought, said and felt in my positive outcome:

What do you think 'self-fulfilling prophecy' means?

2.4 Why is it important to raise our levels of self-esteem?

(Remember, the opposite of low self-esteem is not necessarily high self-esteem. It may be simply accepting and liking yourself – a healthy sense of self-worth and ability.)

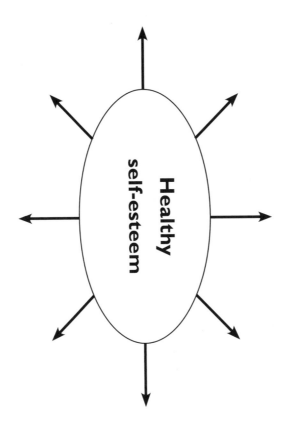

Healthy self-esteem

2.5 An image of healthy self-esteem

What is the quality of healthy self-esteem for you? Sit quietly for a moment with your eyes closed and allow your imagination to come up with an image that somehow represents healthy self-esteem. It could be an animal, an object, a plant, a colour – anything at all. Try not to think about this in any logical sense – just allow an image to 'appear' in your mind. Examine this image from all angles. What are its qualities? Now allow your imagination to take one step further – imagine that you can become this image. Step into being the image. As this image, ask yourself the following questions:

- What is it like to be me (the image)?

- What do I feel physically?

- What do I feel emotionally?

- What do I feel mentally?

- What is the best thing about being this image?

- As this image, what would I most like to happen next?

- What advice do I have for 'self'?

When you are ready, draw or make notes about your image as a reminder of some of the important elements of healthy self-esteem.

2.6 Personal checklist

Shade in the boxes to show how much each of these statements is true for you.

I have a strong sense of who I am	I am very aware of how I behave in different ways according to the situation I am in	I have a good understanding of how different relationships work	I am able to be independent and self-reliant
I am able to be in a relationship without feeling swamped or overwhelmed by the other person	I can usually see things from other people's perspectives	I am usually realistic about how I think others view me	I am respectful and tolerant of other people's views
I understand my emotions and why I feel the way I do in different situations	I feel in control of how I express my emotions	I am able to distinguish my feelings from those of others	I am able to acknowledge my own strengths
I believe that I am a likeable and worthwhile person	I recognize areas that I find difficult and may want to work on	I can accept constructive criticism from others	I am assertive in the way that I deal with unjustified criticism from others
I can tolerate my own mistakes	I like and respect myself	I feel OK about my physical appearance	I take good care of myself
I know how to relax and enjoy myself	I am self-motivated. I tend not to worry too much what others might think of me	I am able to adjust my actions, feelings and thoughts according to realistic assessments of my progress	I believe that I have mastery over my life
I enjoy new challenges	I believe that I let other people see who I really am through my words and actions	I am usually able to listen well to what others have to say	I enjoy talking to new people

2.6 Personal checklist (continued)

I consider myself to be a creative person	I believe that my opinions, thoughts and actions have value	I am confident enough in my own abilities to be able to try different ways of solving problems	I am generally optimistic
I tend not to dwell on past events or worry about the future	I regularly set myself realistic yet challenging goals	I cope well with unexpected events	I believe that I am capable of fulfilling my potential
I often feel inspired through my relationships with others or with music, art or nature	I am able to live with a degree of uncertainty and 'not knowing' in life	I am aware of the power of my imagination and how I can use this to nurture my sense of self and to develop as a person	Bonus Box

The Iceberg of Self-Esteem

Many difficulties can be looked at in terms of an iceberg.

There are parts of a difficulty that can be heard and seen. These overt aspects are equivalent to the part of an iceberg that lies above the water.

When a person is coping with a difficulty there are usually many things going on below the surface too. These covert aspects might include the physical feelings associated with the problem as well as the emotions involved.

Both parts of the iceberg need to be 'melted' or 'chipped away' in order to achieve long-term gains.

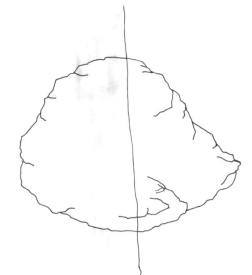

2.7 My personal iceberg of self-esteem

Overt

Covert

2.8 Summary

What I understand about self-esteem:

_____

What I understand about my own self-esteem:

_____

My positive intention is:

_____

_____

You are now going to spend some time thinking in more detail about your self-concept. Remember, this is the overall view that you have of yourself, including your appearance, abilities, attitudes and beliefs.

Section 3

Who Am I?

Aims of this section

- to explore self-perceptions

- to extend the use of imagery as a self-help tool

- to encourage each person to recognize the important stages in their life journey so far

Information and activity sheets

3.1 WHO AM I? (PAGE 98)

This sheet is to be completed individually or in pairs. Invite discussion about what people think makes us who we are. Are group members able to identify any unique characteristics about themselves that are not shared by any other member of the group?

INFORMATION SHEET 3A: KNOWING MY BRAIN (PAGE 99)

This sheet can be used throughout the course when referring to information contained in the 'neuro nuggets' that I have included here and in the facilitator notes for other sections. Demystifying some of the functions of the brain can be an important part of a self-esteem course, helping participants to deepen their understanding of how and why they sometimes feel and act in certain ways.

Suggested reading
Morgan, N. (2005) *Blame my Brain: The Amazing Teenage Brain Revealed.* London: Walker Books.
Nunn, K., Hanstock, T. and Lask, B. (2008) *Who's Who of the Brain.* London: Jessica Kingsley Publishers.

Neuro nugget

The brain really does seem to work on a 'use it or lose it' principle but in a remarkable way. Around 95 per cent of the brain has developed by the age of six but the 'thinking' part of the brain — that part that is involved in decision-making, problem-solving, reasoning and so on — continues to change throughout childhood and into our early twenties. Most notably, there is a second spurt of brain development which peaks at puberty (around 11 or 12 years). This growth spurt results in the brain producing far more cells and connections than can possibly be maintained, so the growth is followed by a 'pruning' of connections (neuroscientists refer to this process as akin to pruning the branches of a tree). This therefore appears to be the optimum time for individuals to strengthen their skills in specialized areas. If an adolescent is going to pursue sport or music for example, certain connections will be strengthened and others will die off. It is a time of great potential, but can also be a time of great confusion!

3.2 CHARACTER SKETCH (PAGE 100)

This is an adaptation of an exercise from Personal Construct Therapy (Kelly 1955; Dalton and Dunnett 1990). It is sometimes difficult for someone with low self-esteem to conceive of how others might see them in a positive, supportive way. They may be tempted to stick to concrete things like 'She goes to X College', 'He has three children.' You may need to encourage a broader explanation of thoughts, values and feelings as well. The character sketch can be used to help the writer to identify 'themes' that might indicate particular areas of concern for them (or hidden strengths).

You could also extend this activity into thinking about how the 'character' might progress during the course of the play. If it is a three act play spanning a two year period how will the character be different in act three? What will he have learned? What will he be doing? How will his life have changed? What happens in act two that facilitates these changes?

Writing a second character sketch of 'future self' can help to focus a person on his goals and might also help him to identify those that are realistically achievable in the short term (see also activity 9.9, page 219).

3.3 IMAGINE THAT! (PAGE 101, ADAPTED FROM 'THE IMAGE AS LIFE METAPHOR' EXERCISE BY DINA GLOUBERMAN 2003, PAGES 94–116)

Lead the whole group through the imagery exercise given below, following the guidelines for previous exercises (e.g. activity sheet 2.2). Before you start the Imagework ensure that everyone knows that they will be exploring an image of a positive quality or aspect of themselves. For someone with chronic low self-esteem, this can seem a difficult task. Reassure everyone that we are simply looking for an unconscious 'resource'. Participants should 'allow' an image to emerge rather than try to think of one before the exercise begins.

Leave plenty of time (at least one hour) for discussion in pairs and in the whole group at the end. This can be a very powerful experience for some people. It is important to recognize that whatever image emerges for an individual is OK. It is simply indicating how that person is feeling about herself and her life at this particular point and it is likely to give her some insight into resources that will help her to move forward. Although you will have specifically set this exercise up to be an exploration of a strength or a 'liked' quality, if it has been an uncomfortable experience for anyone then it is particularly important that she is given the chance to talk it through with the group afterwards.

When you are ready, settle yourself in a comfortable position and allow your eyes to close. Breathe slowly and deeply three times – in through your nose and out through your mouth. Then forget about your breathing. As your mind and body start to relax, allow an image to emerge that somehow represents the best part of who you are. This image could be an animal, an object, a plant or bird or a colour. Just let an image appear in your mind and go with whatever comes for you.

When you have an image, allow yourself to explore it as fully as possible. What does it look like, sound like, feel like? If it can move, how does it move? Imagine that you can take a bird's eye view of this image. As you imagine yourself looking down on it from above, notice its relationship to its environment. Is it alone or with others? Does it seem to 'fit' with its surroundings? What else can you notice?

Now imagine that you can actually become this image so that you can explore it more fully. Step into being this image. Take a breath and really feel how it is to be this image. How does it feel physically, mentally, emotionally? When you feel that you have a sense of what it's like to be this image, ask yourself the following questions:

What are the important qualities of this image?

What is the best thing about being you (the image)?

Is there anything that doesn't feel so good about being you?

What do you hope for as this image?

What do you most need?

What would you like to happen next?

What advice do you have for 'self'?

You may find it useful to have a conversation with 'self'. Swap back and forth between being the image and being 'self' so that you can find out more about what this image means to you and how it represents something important about you.

When you are ready, finish as 'self' and allow the image to fade. Sit quietly for a few moments and think about what the image meant for you. How does this relate to your life and what is happening for you at the moment? What were the important qualities of your image? When you are ready open your eyes and draw or write about your image.

3.4 MY LIFE PATH SO FAR (PAGE 102)

Share the completed activity sheets in pairs. The listener can ask questions for clarification but not as a 'fact-finding' mission!

The different signs could be called anything at all – independence, new job, family, joy, status quo, stagnation; each one is a possible choice for the future.

A note here about adolescence. The adolescent years herald the deepening of the skills of cognitive abstraction: the ability to make informed hypotheses and to realize that what happens today has consequences for the future. It is important for all of us to pause at times and take stock of where we are and where we have come from and to recognize that we have choices about where we go next. For an adolescent who has low self-esteem this can be a particularly scary thought. You need to ensure in this exercise that each person has at least one positive choice on their signposts. If someone is having difficulty seeing a positive direction remind her that the crossroads is a place where she can pause and reflect; that if one or more of the signposts are unclear then it is likely that they will become more recognizable as she starts to set more goals for herself; and that just because we choose a certain path to begin with doesn't mean we have to stay on it, particularly if it is detrimental to our wellbeing. There is an Imagework exercise for exploring life paths. I have not included it here but you may like to experience this for yourself (see Glouberman 2003, pages 173–191).

3.5 SAME AND DIFFERENT (PAGE 103)

Discuss the introduction to this activity sheet and explore the idea that we may do or say things to try and 'fit in' with others. Explore the benefits and drawbacks of this.

Discuss the point that sometimes we admire traits in others that we already have ourselves, although not necessarily to the same degree. We can also choose to develop certain qualities. You might also bring up the point that sometimes what we don't like in others may be a reflection of a similar trait in ourselves.

Making a list of 'things in common' will help participants to identify or clarify their own beliefs, attitudes, preferences and so on.

3.6 ME, MY FAMILY AND MY COMMUNITY (PAGE 104)

This is another way of exploring self-concept in relation to others and of identifying possible ways in which the dynamics of a group might change. If I were to place myself somewhere different what would happen in the rest of the group? Where would I most like to be? Is this possible? How might I start to work towards this?

Geoff, who was taking part in a stroke rehabilitation group, placed himself on the very edge of the group circle. When asked where he would like to be, he indicated a place just outside the circle. Geoff told us that he felt very much a part of the group but knew that he was making a rapid recovery and that he would soon need to move away from the group support and 'go it alone'.

Martin placed himself in the centre of the circle for a self-help group. He felt that other group members looked to him as a role model and he enjoyed the opportunity to support others. He expressed anxiety about the possibility of re-positioning himself nearer the edge of the circle as he felt this would indicate that he had lost his purpose in the group.

3.7 SUMMARY (PAGE 105)

See notes for the summary sheet in Section 2 (page 78).

3.1 Who am I?

Something important about me	Physical features
Personality	Beliefs
Talents and skills	Things I enjoy
Things I dislike	Important events
Important people	Important places
Difficulties I have overcome	Hopes/ambitions
Anything else?	

Knowing My Brain

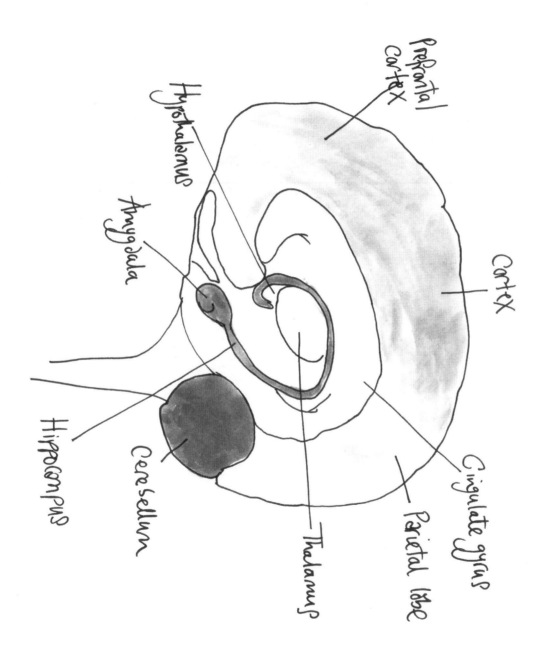

Prefrontal Cortex

Cortex

Hypothalamus

Amygdala

Cingulate gyrus

Parietal lobe

Thalamus

Cerebellum

Hippocampus

3.2 Character sketch

Imagine that you are writing a script for a play about your life. How would you describe yourself in a character sketch? Write as though you are your own best friend, someone who knows you better than anyone else and is supporting and understanding of the true you. Start with your name.

_____ is

Now give your play a title: _____

3.3 Imagine that!

Your group leader will talk you through an imagery exercise. This sheet is for you to record your experience of the exercise.

3.4 My life path so far

Imagine that you could represent your life as a path that you've travelled along from your birth to the present day. Imagine what this path looks like. Is it smooth or does it have 'rocky' patches? Are there bridges? Valleys? Lakes? Woods? Crossroads? Take some time to draw your life path, marking on it any important events. As you draw your path, think about how you have felt physically, mentally and emotionally as you travelled.

When you get to the present day on your life path imagine that you have reached a crossroads. Add a signpost to your drawing to show possible future paths.

Do you have an idea about what the different directions might be called?

3.5 Same and different

Although each of us is a unique individual we do, of course, have things in common with others as well. Our need to feel part of a group or community may lead us to actively seek out like-minded people. Feeling part of a group and being accepted and appreciated by a group gives us a sense of belonging and helps us to feel good about ourselves, especially when our internal reserves are low. Sometimes, however, we may find ourselves behaving in ways that don't truly reflect our self-concept in order to *appear* to fit in with a group. If you have ever found yourself in this situation you will know how uncomfortable it can feel. In the long term this can lead to a lowering of self-esteem rather than an increase.

Think of someone you know who you consider to be like-minded. What things do you have in common? How are you different?

Now think of someone else who you admire. List ten qualities that you admire in them.

Which of these admired qualities do you have?

3.6 Me, my family and my community

Where do you 'fit' with others? Imagine that the circle below represents a group of your family or friends. Who, if anyone, would you place at the centre of the circle? Where would the other people be in relation to each other and in relation to the centre? Where would you place yourself at the moment? Is this where you want to be? If not, put yourself where you would feel more comfortable.

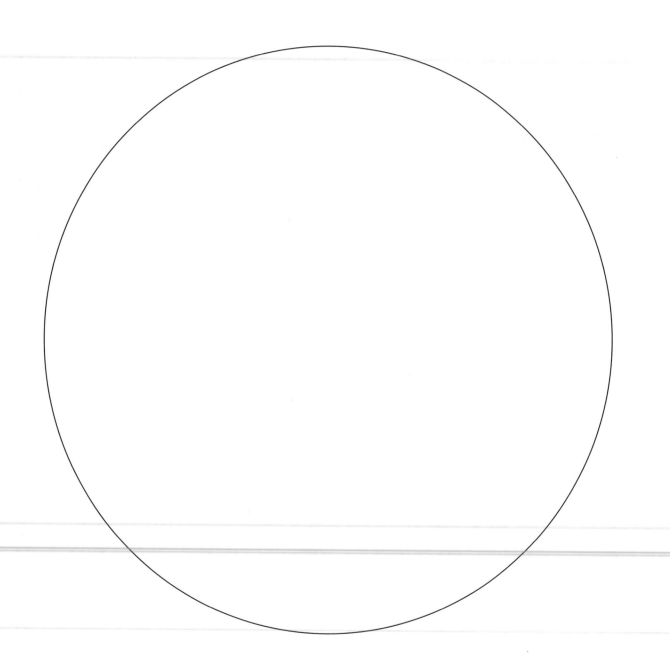

3.7 Summary

What I understand about self-concept:

_____

_____

My positive intention is:

_____

What I understand about my own self-concept:

_____

_____

You are now going to spend some time exploring self-awareness. This includes being focused in the 'here and now' and understanding more about your own emotions.

Section 4

Self-Awareness

Aims of this section

- to learn the process of focusing
- to deepen awareness of emotions and how we express these
- to explore the use of imagery in helping to create desired feeling 'states'

Information and activity sheets

INFORMATION SHEET 4A: BEING SELF-AWARE (PAGE 113)

This is for discussion in the whole group.

Suggested reading

Kabat-Zinn, J. (1996) *Full Catastrophe Living: How to Cope with Stress, Pain and Illness Using Mindfulness Meditation.* London: Piatkus.

Stevens, J. O. (1989) *Awareness.* London: Eden Grove.

4.1 FOCUSING (PAGES 114–5)

Focusing can be done seated or lying down.

Lead the whole group in this exercise. Leave plenty of time at the end for people to share their experiences of focusing. Encourage participants to ask themselves questions such as:

- What do I tend to think about when my attention is not focused?
- Am I able to redirect my focus of attention?
- Do I find myself worrying about 'getting it right'?
- Do I find the process easy or difficult? Why might that be?

The inter-relatedness of focusing, concentrating and self-calming has been written about extensively. We know, for example, that regular use of some forms of meditative practice, where an individual focuses on one particular stimulus such as a sound/word (mantra), a visual stimulus such as a light, or a kinaesthetic stimulus such as following his or her own breathing pattern, can have positive benefits for people experiencing mental health difficulties and can enhance pain control (Kabat-Zinn 1996). The effective use of meditation causes the body to release natural opioids into the bloodstream resulting in the subjective experience of feeling calm.

The benefits of undertaking a regular period of focusing go beyond relaxation however. It is also a way of training the mind to leave behind worries and concerns and be more aware of the present moment.

Each of us selectively attends to different stimuli throughout the day, shifting our awareness from external sights, sounds and smells to internal thoughts and feelings, and changing our level of engagement with tasks in response to such dimensions as the strength of the stimulus, our personal needs and preferences at the time or our motivation to attend. These processes are a natural part of our lives, and ones which we can easily take for granted because they are often largely unconscious. Even while reading this page you will undoubtedly have switched from focusing on the written words to an internal thought and will have simultaneously filtered out extraneous stimuli such as a clock ticking in the room or the sound of traffic outside (and in reading that, you may well have suddenly noticed these noises!).

Redirecting our attention can be made much more conscious. We can choose *where* to direct our awareness and we can learn *how* to direct it. When we know how to direct our attention effectively we can, for example, notice and then change an unwanted internal stimulus (e.g. unnecessary muscle tension or a thought that is causing us to feel anxious); we can notice and value intuitive feelings and ideas; we can filter out unnecessary stimuli that might interfere with concentration on a task; and we can notice the smallest of details in our environment or choose to take a wider view. In so doing, we are basically choosing to give emphasis to different areas of our experience. We are not denying or belittling the existence of other dimensions of that experience, simply deciding to put our focus and energies into one aspect.

The ability to maintain focus through a degree of self-awareness and self-control leads to concentration, and effective concentration contributes to perseverance. When we concentrate, we put energy into action, or, as the philosopher Keyserling said:

The ability to concentrate is a real propelling power of the totality of our psychic mechanism. Nothing elevates our capacity of action more than its development. Any success, no matter in which area, can be explained by the intelligent use of this capacity. (Keyserling quoted in Ferrucci 1982, page 30)

We can also learn to consciously adapt to changing stimuli. Adaptability enables us to move from one focus of attention to another appropriately and allows us to attend to more than one stimulus at the same time. Often this divided attention is a mixture of an internal stimulus (e.g. a memory) and an external stimulus. So for example, we can link a current challenging event with the memory of a similar past experience that we handled well in order to feel confident about coping with it effectively again this time.

Neuro nugget

The adolescent brain is still developing the capacity for focused, sustained and divided attention. Learning this conscious control is undoubtedly a complex process. It appears that different aspects of attention involve distinct areas of the brain. The parietal lobe, for example, is active in selective attention (focusing on specific aspects of the environment) and in shifting attention from one aspect to another. This information is then passed to the cingulate gyrus (which stretches from the front to the back of the brain) and to the frontal lobes. The cingulate gyrus is responsible for filtering out irrelevant information (selective attention) and for sustaining attention on one stimulus over another. The frontal lobes are vital to the formation of our personality and perform many different functions. With regard to attention, they perform a supervisory role. For example, they enable flexible thinking and the ability to focus on more than one task at the same time (Nunn, Hanstock and Lask 2008).

The pre-frontal cortex, as its name suggests, constitutes the front part of the frontal lobes. The right pre-frontal cortex plays a part in our capacity to deliberately direct our attention and in the phenomenon of 'attention fatigue' (Glosser and Goodglass 1990). When we have been attending to something for a sustained period of time (perhaps a difficult puzzle, a new skill, a complex problem-solving activity) this area of the brain appears to reach a maximum capacity point in its ability to help us to filter out unnecessary or distracting stimuli that are not relevant to the task. In effect it ceases to function efficiently for short periods of time making it more and more difficult to pay attention and also more difficult to inhibit impulsivity.

INFORMATION SHEET 4B: AWARENESS OF EMOTIONS (PAGE 116)

Discuss how people experience different emotions and how we might suppress our emotions if we think we should be able to cope, or it's wrong to express anger or to cry and so on. When this happens then there is no appropriate action for people to respond to. Others may not realize how we feel and therefore continue to act in ways that reinforce our original emotions. By learning to value our feelings and by facing difficult or confusing situations and coping with them successfully, we will be able to confidently and creatively meet new challenges and develop our skills, so further strengthening feelings of wellbeing. We will also develop a healthy level of 'emotional resilience': the ability to cope with temporary feelings of helplessness, frustration or upset without being engulfed by them or experiencing them as failure.

Neuro nugget

One of the primary developmental tasks in the emotional life of a young child is the establishment of an effective emotion-regulation system: the ability to self-regulate and self-calm so that they are not constantly overwhelmed with difficult emotions. There are two areas of the brain that are particularly important in the development of this self-regulatory capacity: the amygdala and the pre-frontal cortex. The amygdala is a small almond-shaped area of interconnected structures located on each side of the brain within the temporal lobes. This area plays a major part in how we experience emotions and is responsible for detecting threat and initiating the stress response (fight, flight or freeze) by sending information to the hypothalamus (which is concerned with regulating various systems within the body, including the release of stress hormones). The amygdala has been shown to be involved in the laying down of immediate and long-lasting emotional memories associated with perceived threat. For example, when a person or object is associated (even by chance) with a traumatic event, the amygdala will produce such a strong neuronal response that a future encounter with that same person or object will trigger the stress response regardless of any actual threat being present (Nunn, Hanstock and Lask 2008, pages 137–8).

The amygdala's primitive and rapid response to threat is, however, mediated by other areas of the brain, for example the pre-frontal cortex which deals with feelings and social interactions. Once the system of connections has developed and is working well, impulsive reactions to perceived threat can be inhibited or regulated via the 'thinking' processes carried out at this higher level, thereby preventing us from being overwhelmed, for example by inappropriate fear and anxiety.

Young adolescents tend to be very emotionally labile. As we have seen, this is partly due to neurological development and hormonal changes but is also often due to the fact that they haven't yet built up enough experience to be able to predict how long things will last or to have developed enough successful coping strategies. They may sometimes need 'permission' to feel what they are feeling and assurance that all emotions are valid and that we can learn strategies to reduce the intensity of some of them. Some young people (as well as some adults) are very unaware of what exactly it is that they are feeling or why they are feeling it. If they feel swamped with emotion they may 'shut down' as a self-protection.

For all these reasons, a sensitive, structured exploration of feelings and how we express them needs to be incorporated into any self-esteem course.

4.2 HOW I NORMALLY EXPRESS EMOTIONS (PAGE 117)

Brainstorm emotions first. Remember to include 'feel-good' emotions in the list. The activity sheet can be completed individually or in discussion with a partner. The points can then be explored more generally (rather than in relation to a particular person) in the whole group. It is important to discuss what happens as a consequence of the way we choose to express our emotions: how others respond and why; how we feel afterwards and so on.

4.3 STATE MANAGEMENT (PAGES 118–9)

This is an amalgam of exercises from Neurolinguistic Programming and Imagework.

'Negative' states are quite easy to manufacture! If someone tells me that I will have to introduce myself to a group in a foreign language and I have only a few minutes to learn how to do it, I am sure that I would experience a state of anxiety. If I was then told that I could do it in English if I wished, my anxiety would subside. My anticipation of what might happen if I attempted a foreign language could cause my body to produce an anxiety state. This link between mind and body can also be demonstrated by getting the group to imagine themselves cutting a slice of lemon and then sucking on it. If you elaborate the picture enough – 'Imagine that you can see the spurt of lemon juice as you slice into the lemon', etc. – the majority of the group will undoubtedly experience a rush of saliva or will indicate a sense of the sour taste by their facial expression.

The unconscious mind believes the images that we form of ourselves as if they were already reality. If we can 'manufacture' a positive experience and make it vivid enough in our imagination then we generally start to act in the real world as though the desired change had already taken place.

I suggest that you demonstrate the state management exercise with just one person from the group and then invite the group to facilitate each other in pairs. It is important to encourage peer facilitation as early as possible in the course to reinforce the idea that individuals will be able to use these exercises on their own or with another group member after the course has finished.

4.4 CONFIDENCE (PAGE 120) AND 4.5 RECREATING A MEMORY (PAGE 121)

These activities provide further opportunities for the group to facilitate each other after a demonstration. Sometimes people worry that the first of these exercises isn't 'real', that guessing how someone else might feel when they are confident won't help them to be confident in real life. It's important to explore the idea that we all 'act' in different ways according to who we are with and according to the situation. Acting 'as if' we were someone else for a short period simply gives us the opportunity to explore how things would be if we chose to do things differently; it highlights that we have a choice in how we think and behave.

4.6 SUMMARY (PAGE 122)

See notes for the summary sheet in Section 2 (page 78).

Section 4

Self-Awareness

Being Self-Aware

Self-awareness involves being able to identify your emotions and understand the reasons why you feel the way you do in different situations. It also involves an awareness of your body and the way in which your thoughts can affect you physically.

Perhaps there have been times when you have imagined something so clearly that it has felt as though it was actually happening. This could, of course, be a pleasant experience but you may find yourself more frequently thinking about negative things. The fear, anxiety, tension or worry that you experience at these times can feel very real. This is partly because the imagination directly affects the autonomic nervous system — that part of our nervous system that controls such things as heart rate, breathing and blood pressure. So thinking about what might go wrong in your life actually causes your body to react as though you were already facing that difficult situation: your imagination acts as a connecting system — it connects your mind, body and emotions.

Your imagination is also setting up a 'blueprint' for trouble. So if you eventually do have to face the situation in reality you already have a 'memory' of it not going well. Telling yourself how badly you are going to cope in this way may therefore lead to actual poor performance — your imagination results in a 'self-fulfilling prophecy'.

For example, if I believe that I am 'shy' or 'clumsy' then I will have images of myself in any situation acting in a 'shy' or 'clumsy' way. I will continue to expect myself to act in this way and my images will strengthen my beliefs about myself.

Fortunately, it is possible to change old image patterns and use the power of the imagination in a positive way to affect our future behaviour and thoughts. You have already started to explore this in some of the exercises you did earlier on in this course.

4.1 Focusing

Focusing involves directing your attention to different areas of your body and just being aware of any sensations. By keeping your attention on physical sensations you are training your mind to be focused in the 'here and now' rather than caught up with thoughts about the future or the past. By observing your body in this way you will also probably find that you naturally allow any areas of tension to relax.

You may want to make your own recording of this exercise. If you do, remember to read the instructions very slowly and calmly with plenty of pauses to allow yourself time to focus fully.

Settle yourself into a comfortable position and allow your eyes to gently close, withdrawing your attention from the outside world. Begin to notice your breathing – without trying to change anything, just noticing the natural pattern as you breathe in and out. You might notice this by being aware of the rise and fall of your stomach or you might be aware of the feel of the air as you breathe in and out through your nose.

Continue to focus on your breathing for a few moments. When other thoughts come into your mind, just acknowledge them and go back to being aware of your breathing…

Now take your attention to your feet. Focus on your feet as though you had never really thought about them before. Notice the sensations in your feet just at this moment. They may feel warm or cool, numb or tingling, painful, tense, relaxed. There is no right or wrong feeling. Whatever is there just notice it.

Now allow your attention to leave your feet and move easily and smoothly to the lower part of your legs. Notice whatever feeling is there just at this moment… Now move up to your knees and the upper half of your legs and notice whatever feeling is there… Now to your hips and lower back…and then gradually along the length of your spine… Begin to notice your shoulders, focus on all the feelings around your shoulders. Notice the back of your shoulders, across the top of your shoulders and down into your arms…

Feel what's happening in your arms… Whatever is there, just notice it… Remember there are no right or wrong feelings. Whatever you can feel is OK…

And now focus on your hands and fingers… Notice the backs of your hands…the palms of your hands…and each of your fingers in turn….

Now the lower half of the front of your body… Move your attention along the front of your body until you reach your chest…and go a little deeper and see if you can notice your heart beat… Again, as other thoughts enter your mind just let them pass through and refocus your attention back to your body… Now to your shoulders again. Be fully aware of your shoulders… Then becoming aware of your neck – the sides of your neck, the back of your neck… Be aware of the sensations in and around your throat…

© Deborah Plummer 2014

4.1 Focusing (continued)

Become aware of your jaw now. Are your teeth pressed together or are they slightly apart so that your jaw is relaxed?... Notice your eyes and the sensations around your eyes... Become aware of your forehead and notice any expression on your face.... Moving your attention now to the top of your head...down the back of your head...and resting once again at your shoulders...

Now instead of thinking of yourself in parts, be aware of your whole body...sensing your whole body...being aware of how sensations change from moment to moment... Continue to focus in this way for a few moments.

Now while still sensing your body, start to listen to whatever sounds there are around you.... Begin to move your hands and feet a little bit.... In a moment you will open your eyes. When you do, focus your gaze on one particular thing in the room and while you look at it, keep sensing your body and listening to the sounds around you.... So, when you feel ready, open your eyes and look at one thing with your full concentration. Now shift your gaze to something else...and come back to the room fully, allowing other thoughts to return. You may want to stretch or shift your position.

What did I learn about myself while I was focusing?

Awareness of Emotions

Do you place different value on different emotions? Perhaps you view some emotions as OK to have and others as not OK. Of course all feelings are real, but perhaps you are more comfortable with some than with others. If we frequently deny or 'bottle up' our feelings they may eventually feel quite uncontrollable. We may also stop trusting ourselves and our own feelings, not even certain how we should be feeling in some situations.

If we are unaware of what we feel then this will also affect how we are with other people. For example, my first feeling after a difficult encounter with someone might be 'I feel bad' but I might express this as anger. Or, if I don't feel comfortable with feelings of anger, I could end up feeling hurt and upset instead, even when anger would have been justified.

It is important to recognize all your emotions and listen to what your body is telling you. Useful, appropriate emotions brought about by realistic thoughts lead to positive action. For example, it may be appropriate to feel anxious about some situations so that you can make sure you are well prepared in advance.

Some emotions can seem overwhelming at times and can stop us from making the changes that we want. However, by changing the way we think about ourselves and about the situation we can often experience different or less intense emotions instead.

One way that we can help ourselves with this is to remember that other people do not control our emotions. I may feel embarrassed or fed up about something but these feelings are my reactions to situations – they can't be forced on me.

We always have choices about how we feel. This also means that we can't assume that others know what we are feeling unless we tell them. They may be able to hazard a guess but could quite easily get it wrong!

4.2 How I normally express emotions

Think about how you normally express your emotions and consider whether or not your responses are always useful/appropriate.

Emotion	How I normally express this emotion	What I experience as a consequence

Is there any specific behaviour from your list that you would like to change and could realistically alter at this stage? Look on this as an experiment. How could you alter a particular way that you express an emotion? What do you anticipate would be the result of this change?

4.3 State management

If we can 'get in a state' over something just by thinking about it, just imagine the benefits of choosing what state we'd like to be in! This really is a possibility. If we can work out exactly what a particular state of feeling is composed of then we can learn to think ourselves into that state at other times.

Every state has very specific elements:

- body posture, muscle tension, breathing, movement
- inner images, feelings and self-talk
- our attitudes, beliefs and values that determine how we experience events.

Identifying the elements of a desirable state, and learning how to recall them when you want to, gives you a valuable personal resource.

For the next exercise you will be asked to think of a time when you have felt particularly happy, peaceful, successful, in control or have experienced any other enjoyable 'state' of being that you would like to reproduce in other circumstances.

The state that I would like to explore in more depth is:

Choose a specific memory of a time when you were in the positive state that you would like to experience more of. Think of the exact moment that was the best part of the whole experience.

1. Imagine that there is a circle in front of you on the floor. This is the circle of calmness, success or whatever state you want to explore. Close your eyes and step into the circle. Imagine yourself as if you were actually in your remembered situation again. Notice the key features of this state. Really breathe into being in this state. Where exactly are you? Who is with you? How are you standing or sitting? What can you see around you? What can you hear? How do you feel? What are you thinking?

2. When you feel that you are experiencing it as fully as possible allow an image to come into your mind that somehow represents this state for you. Perhaps there is also a word or gesture that goes with this state? If so, say the word out loud or make the movement that shows how it is to feel like this.

3. Now physically step out of this state (step out of the circle). Open your eyes, talk about something else or focus your attention on something in the room.

4.3 State management (continued)

4. When you are ready, step back into the circle. Use the image you came up with and/or the word or gesture that links with your positive state. This time you are aiming to experience the state without having to imagine the past event that last triggered it. Repeat steps 3 and 4 two or three times until you feel you can experience your desired state just by using your image and word or gesture.

5. When you are ready, step out of the circle again. Now think of a situation in the near future where you would like to have this positive state.

6. Once more step into the circle and regain your positive state. This time, imagine going into the future event while in this positive state. How do you feel? What is happening? What are you aware of? What are the new possibilities?

When you have finished this exercise, take some time to do a drawing to represent some of your feelings and thoughts or to make notes about what you have experienced.

4.4 Confidence

Loss or lack of self-confidence is usually experienced in relation to specific areas and for a specific reason. I can be confident in one area and not in another.

What does confidence mean to you? Think of someone you admire and who you believe to be very confident. Imagine that they are standing in front of you. What is the first thing that you notice about their appearance? How do you feel when you look at this person?

Now imagine that you can become this person for a few moments. Close your eyes and step into being this confident person. Allow your body posture to change so that you can really get a sense of what it's like to be very confident. What do you notice? As this person, how do you stand, walk, talk? How do you approach others? What do you think about being you? What sort of clothes do you wear? How do you make decisions? What advice do you have for others about building confidence?

It doesn't matter if you don't really know this person well enough to know the true answers to these questions. The idea is to get a strong sense of how someone might experience this level of confidence.

When you feel ready, step back into being you again. Think about what you experienced. Draw or write about the key elements of confidence as you experienced it.

4.5 Recreating a memory

Remember a time when you have felt confident in the past. Where were you? What were you doing? Who were you with? How did you know that you were feeling confident? Be as specific as you can be about how you experienced the feeling of confidence. What did you feel physically? What were your thoughts? If you can create this scene vividly enough in your mind you will be able to recreate the feeling as well.

Make a list of times when you have recognized these feelings. Add to this list when you recognize these feelings again in the next few weeks.

4.6 Summary

What I understand about self-awareness:

What I understand about my own self-awareness:

My positive intention is:

As you have been working through these activity sheets you will have already been making some changes. Perhaps you have begun to think differently about some situations or about yourself. Perhaps you have started to make changes in the way that you respond to some people or situations. To help you to keep these changes working for you, the next section looks at what change is all about.

Section 5

The Challenge of Change

Aims of this section

- to explore the meaning of change in our lives

- to heighten awareness of what helps individuals to make positive changes and of some of the obstacles to change

- to highlight the possibilities of making informed choices about the direction of change

Information and activity sheets

INFORMATION SHEET 5A: DEFINITIONS AND DESCRIPTIONS (PAGE 130)

This is to be discussed in the group.

Discuss the link between Imagework and personal construct theory; imagery can encapsulate constructs and their links remarkably effectively. Images often allow much greater insight than words ever could and Imagework also provides the opportunity to elaborate alternatives, thereby facilitating the process of conscious choice and the possibility of altering our less helpful constructs about ourselves and the world.

Suggested reading

Glouberman, D. (2010) *Life Choices, Life Changes: Develop Your Personal Vision with Imagework.* London: Skyros Books.

Glouberman, D. (2014) *You Are What You Imagine: three steps to a new beginning using Imagework.* London: Watkins Publishing.

Fransella, F. and Dalton, P. (1990) *Personal Construct Counselling in Action.* London: Sage.

5.1 WHAT IS CHANGE? (PAGE 131)

Compare and discuss differing views of change highlighted by the free association exercise. Here are a few examples of how this works:

change – make different – alter – irrevocable – for life

change – different – not the same – unique – a one off – special – stands out from the crowd

change – not the same any more – loss – sadness – yearning – stuck

change – relief – excitement – enthusiasm – energy – leap

5.2 COPING WITH CHANGE (PAGE 132)

Collate any general themes that have been identified.

5.3 MOTIVATION FOR CHANGE (PAGE 133)

Again, this could form the basis for discussion about what motivates different people.

Miller and Rollnick (2002), the proponents of motivational interviewing, highlight three aspects as being primary components of motivation for change. The first is readiness: are we *ready* for this change – is it top of our priority list right now? The second is willingness: to what extent are we *willing* to change (i.e. how much do we desire the change)? And finally, how confident are we that we are *able* to change?

If we are ready, willing and able then this in turn leads to increased engagement with the process of change. If a person is not engaged with the change (for example, if the change is not self-initiated, is not intrinsically rewarding or has no immediate value) then we might predict that learning and generalization will be minimized (see Part I, Chapter 4, 'Learning and Generalizing Knowledge and Skills').

5.4 KEEP IT OR CHANGE IT? (PAGE 134)

This activity sheet could be used as the basis for each group member to take two minutes to 'sell' themselves to the group. The group could also hold an 'auction' of their greatest talents. Encourage use of advertising jargon to make this a fun exercise. I have also used this idea towards the end of a course to have a 'bargain basement' sale of unwanted or now outdated elements.

5.5 MAKING A COMMITMENT (PAGE 135)

Imagining that you have already achieved a goal can be more powerful than planning what you will have to do beforehand. The idea of projecting yourself forward in time to explore a positive outcome is well known in sports psychology – athletes are trained to visualize themselves making the perfect high jump, for example, so that when they come to compete they have a 'memory' of having already achieved their goal. This theme is revisited several times in different sections of this book.

5.6 OBSTACLES IN THE WAY OF CHANGE (PAGE 136) AND INFORMATION SHEET 5B: RESISTING CHANGE (PAGE 137)

The aim here is to help participants to recognize that there are very real reasons why change might be difficult. Building self-esteem involves tackling some of these obstacles but also involves recognition that their original purpose might have been self-protection. This means that we need to allow participants the opportunity to work through any resistances in their own time. Obstacles are usually the best indicator of the most appropriate solution and this is often clearly illustrated in Imagework. The following is an example of how this might work.

Sarah had great difficulty in making friends at her new school. Her attempts to engage in conversation with her peers were awkward and frequently misconstrued as interference. She was seen as 'different' and experienced people's reactions to her as rejection. Before long she gave up attempting to join in and would simply watch from the sidelines. During an Imagework exercise Sarah saw herself behind a huge brick wall. She could hear her classmates on the other side and she could sometimes see them through a little peep hole, but they could no longer see her. The brick wall felt strong and protective, shielding her from harm. Removing this wall would undoubtedly have been far too devastating for her and yet the protection was also compounding her isolation. If the wall was to be taken down she felt that she would need someone to help her and it would have to be very gradual so as to prevent it from collapsing completely and causing damage to herself. Sarah came up with a creative alternative. She found that, in fact, the wall was not attached to anything at one end and would therefore allow her to make short forays to the other side and retain the possibility of a quick return if needed. She could also invite one other person to join her behind the wall to take part in a conversation on a topic of Sarah's choosing and then accompany this person back to the main group. Neither of these solutions need to be analysed although the practicalities of what she was suggesting could be discussed if appropriate (Who would you choose for this conversation? How would you approach them? What would you say? What is your 'get out' strategy? And so on).

When we can see the reasons for resistance to change we are in a better position to be able to choose more useful strategies for looking after ourselves: strategies that will support the change process rather than hinder it (see Part I, Chapter 2, 'Self-Esteem, Learning and the Process of Change').

Another image that could be explored in the context of change is the image of the internal saboteur – that part of us that appears to thwart our attempts at change. The following illustrates one of those 'aha' moments experienced by a client during this imagery (Plummer 2013, page 355).

M's saboteur image was a mischievous little girl who would go to great lengths to 'trip up' M and prevent her from trying new things in life. When M became the little girl and explored her relationship with this saboteur she discovered two important aspects. Firstly, this was a little girl's best attempts at self-protection, and secondly there was a positive 'playful' side to the image which could be utilized in a different way, allowing M to play with trying new approaches and new experiences without so much fear of making mistakes or failing.

5.7 WORKING ON AVOIDANCES (PAGE 138)

Avoidance is fed by fear and fear is increased by avoidance! Most people need to work on their avoidances in a structured way so that they feel that each step is manageable. See also Section 11, 'Setting and Achieving Goals'.

INFORMATION SHEET 5C: DESENSITIZATION (PAGE 139)

This is for discussion in the whole group.

5.8 DESENSITIZATION (PAGE 140)

At this point you could introduce the idea of group members suggesting small challenges for each other.

5.9 TAKING WORTHWHILE RISKS (PAGE 141)

Discuss worthwhile risks that participants have taken in the past, both large and small. Every change involves a risk of some sort. Some suggestions for minimizing the difficulties involved in taking a risk might be:

- invest time in researching the risk

- only tackle one risk at a time

- start with small goals

- believe in yourself

- believe that the risk is worth taking

- seek support from someone who has already taken a similar risk

- resolve to accept the worst outcome should it happen

- do everything possible to make sure that the worst doesn't happen.

5.10 THE ABC OF CHANGE (PAGE 142)

This model comes from Personal Construct Therapy. It is a technique originally outlined by Finn Tschudi (Dalton and Dunnett 1990). Tschudi's model is described as being 'useful in exploring the reasons behind not moving from one pole of a construct to another apparently more attractive one, or for examining difficulties in making a decision between two alternatives' (Dalton and Dunnett 1990, page 89). This can be demonstrated as a group decision-making process. For example, you could explore the pros and cons of using a regular relaxation technique. The following is an example explored by a group of adults who stammer.

A1 Stammering openly, no techniques used	A2 Using some form of fluency control
Disadvantages	Advantages
1. Can lead to frustration if attitude to stammering does not change	1. Gives another option (more choice)
2. Feeling out of control	2. Helps to keep focus on what you're doing
3. Increased avoidance (unless attitude changes)	3. Increased fluency
4. Difficult to set other goals related to speech	4. Feeling as though 'dealing' with the problem
5. Affects confidence	5. Helps to expand 'comfort zone'
6. Possibly reinforces stammering behaviour	6. Helps reduce avoidances
	7. Helps you to feel more positive
	8. Can set goals related to process

A1 Stammering openly, no techniques used	A2 Using some form of fluency control
Advantages	Disadvantages
1. If more relaxed about stammering can keep things in perspective	1. Focusing on fluency techniques could 'take over' life
2. Tolerance of occasional stammers and feeling that coping well with these can increase self-esteem and confidence	2. Pressure to keep up the 'front' of being a fluent person all the time
3. Showing that you accept it will get positive reactions from others	3. Becoming reliant on it as a prop
4. Stammer becomes more relaxed when not fighting it or trying to cover it up	4. Hard work. Lots of thinking time
5. Less effort in terms of time needed to 'practise'	5. Fitting the practice into a busy life (i.e. not keeping it in perspective)
	6. Intolerance of occasional stammers could lead to more anxiety

5.11 SUMMARY (PAGE 143)

See notes for the summary sheet, Section 2 (page 78).

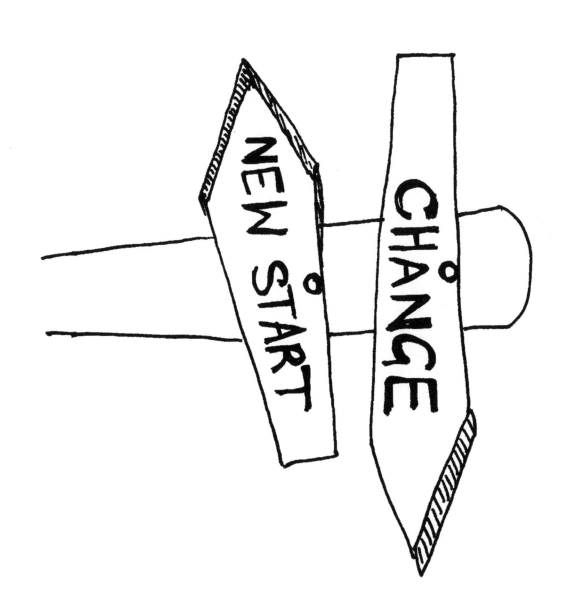

Definitions and Descriptions

Personal construct theory

American psychologist George Kelly outlined a theory of personal development which we can use to help us to understand how we make sense of the world and how we deal with change.

Kelly suggested that each of us is like a scientist: we look for patterns in how the world works then we make hypotheses (form beliefs about the world and ourselves) and test these out by 'experimenting'. Sometimes our experiments seem to prove our hypotheses and so strengthen our belief system. At other times our experiments don't turn out the way we expected so then we either alter our beliefs or alter our experiment. In this way we have the potential for constantly 'reinventing' ourselves.

As our beliefs are formulated and strengthened we start to predict or anticipate events. These anticipations determine what we do and think. So if we form some beliefs that are not useful to us we may continue to act and think in ways that hold back our progress.

Imagework

Imagework is the term created by Dr Dina Glouberman to describe the methods she has developed for using imagery to understand and change our lives.

Each person's imagery is unique to them. It represents our own personal way of relating to ourselves and the world: our own personal way of thinking. We can use imagery to come to a better understanding of our beliefs and to formulate new beliefs that will give us more choices about how we lead our lives and enable us to create a more positive future for ourselves.

5.1 What is change?

We are all constantly changing, constantly recreating ourselves. This is inevitable. We cannot *not* change!

Every day we experience new situations, meet new people, hear or read new information and then we adjust our emotions, reactions, memories, knowledge store and so on.

Building self-esteem involves several changes. For example:

- changes in the way that you see yourself in difficult situations and in the way that you react in these situations

- a change in attitude about the part played by other people in the maintenance of your self-esteem

- a change in the way others react to you as you try out more new things

- a change in your general lifestyle as you try out different and more effective ways of handling people and events

- a physical change as you alter such things as habitual muscle tension.

Free Association

On a large sheet of paper write down the word 'change'. Next to this write the first word that comes to mind that you associate with change. Now write a third word which immediately comes to mind in relation to the second, a fourth which relates to the third and so on.

Keep writing as fast as you can, putting down the first word or phrase you think of each time. Only stop when you have about ten words/phrases or when you are starting to repeat what you have already written.

When you have completed your own free association exercise discuss this with one other person. How do your words differ from theirs? How are they alike? Have you discovered anything about how you view the process of change in your own life?

5.2 Coping with change

Think of a time in your life when you have made a change of some sort. This may have been through your own choice or through circumstances that were not in your control.

- What was it that you changed?
- Why did you make this change?
- How did the change happen?
- How long did it take?
- How did you feel about it?
- Was there anyone else involved?
- Did you plan beforehand?
- What happened afterwards?
- Did this change trigger any other changes?
- Was it an enjoyable change?
- Were there any surprises?
- Were there any disappointments?
- Is there anything you would like to have done differently?

Discuss this with one other person in the group. Do you have anything in common in how you cope with change?

Have you discovered anything about what you personally need to have or need to know in order to make the changes that you want?

5.3 Motivation for change

Why do people make changes? Knowing what motivates you to change can help you to make more conscious choices about the way that you change and will help in the long-term maintenance of change.

Make a list of things which might motivate you to make changes in your life such as having fun, being popular, relationships with others or personal success.

Put them in order of importance to you.

5.4 Keep it or change it?

Imagine that you could buy, sell or exchange some things about yourself. What would you buy more of? What would you sell? What would you happily exchange and what would you want to exchange it for? What would you definitely want to keep?

I would sell:

I would keep:

I would buy:

I would exchange:

5.5 Making a commitment

Write down one small thing that you would like to change.

How would making this change be of benefit to you?

Imagine that this change has already taken place. You are already benefiting from having made this change. How are you different? What is happening in your life? How do you feel? How do other people know that you have made this change? What, if anything, was difficult and how did you overcome the difficulty? What are you most pleased about with regard to this change? What will happen next?

5.6 Obstacles in the way of change

Deciding on a goal and realizing the benefits of achieving that goal are an important first step, but why is it that so many of us never get any further than this? Let's now look at the way we often resist change in our lives.

What do you consider to be 'obstacles' to change? What might prevent you from making the changes that you want?

Resisting Change

Change can be rewarding and stimulating but also daunting because of the element of the unknown. Sometimes we resist change even though we know it might be of benefit to us. George Kelly identified several possible factors that might influence this resistance. Here are four of them:

Threat

Kelly defined threat as the awareness of an imminent change in our central or 'core' constructs. Our core constructs are the most resistant to change because they define the very core of how we see ourselves: the most important aspects of how we make sense of the world. We don't want this change to happen so we may try to avoid or sabotage change. Threat is extremely uncomfortable. You may experience the sensations associated with panic or anger.

Fear

This is described as an awareness of an imminent but smaller change. It is not as strong a feeling as threat but can still be disagreeable.

Anxiety

This happens when we are faced with an event that has not been part of our previous experience so we can't accurately predict what is going to happen.

Guilt

Guilt feelings arise when we feel we are about to, or have already, stepped outside the 'core' role structure that we have invented for ourselves (i.e. a person's own standards of behaviour, not social or cultural codes).

Kelly argued that the way to overcome these feelings is to actively 'experiment' so that we can increase the range of our experiences. If we don't experiment (take action) we will perhaps try to keep our world small and manageable, avoiding changes because of fear, anxiety, guilt or feeling of threat. We will tend to stay with or return to what we know best because from that standpoint we are able to predict outcomes (even though what we know best may be harmful to our physical, emotional, mental or spiritual wellbeing). It takes an investment of time and courage to move away from this habitual pattern and to replace it with new ways of acting and thinking.

5.7 Working on avoidances

Make a list of any situations, people, feelings or relationships that you know you try to avoid.

Think about why you avoid. What do you fear happening?

What benefits do you experience by avoiding?

Choose one thing that you are going to approach rather than avoid. What is the worst thing that could happen? How will you minimize the chances of this happening? What previous positive experience can you draw on to help you?

Desensitization

Becoming more desensitized to difficult situations is an ongoing process rather than a separate phase of building self-esteem. Desensitization in this context doesn't mean becoming 'numb' or unaware of your feelings. When self-esteem is low we may become acutely sensitive to other people's reactions to us and constantly plagued by worries about what they may think of us. Desensitization is about making realistic assessments of situations and not allowing adverse responses to worry us too much.

For example, if you feel uncomfortable in groups, when you enter a situation where you may be called on to speak you could find yourself thinking 'Should I speak or should I stay quiet?' You may then start to worry that if you do speak, others may not find what you have to say interesting. You may end up saying little or missing the opportunity to say what you wanted.

This approach/avoidance dilemma results in anxiety and physical tension. For some people, when they do speak they then blush or are very hesitant and this increases the approach/avoidance dilemma.

We all avoid doing things from time to time, perhaps because we have no motivation for doing them or perhaps because we fear the consequences of having a go. You may have found that over the years you have built up a series of strategies to avoid certain feelings, situations or people.

Unfortunately, the more that we avoid something because we fear it, the more the fear builds up until it eventually dominates much of how we think and act.

One of the biggest steps forward in building your self-esteem is to begin to eliminate avoidance strategies. The more you face your worries head on, the more easily you will be able to cope with them.

5.8 Desensitization

What does the term 'desensitization' mean to you?

What are the benefits of becoming more desensitized to difficult situations?

List some possible ways of helping yourself to become more desensitized. Choose one thing that you will do during the next week.

5.9 Taking worthwhile risks

Many of us have a fear of having to deal with rejection or failure if we attempt to make changes. We may decide not to even try and because we don't try we will build up more and more fear about the situation because we have no experience from which we can predict how things might turn out. In a sense, every change involves a risk but taking that risk reduces the fear.

Our imagination can always come up with worse scenarios than need ever happen. So once you have decided to take a risk of some sort remember to visualize a positive outcome!

Make a list of the ways in which you could lessen the possible difficulties involved in taking a risk.

5.10 The ABC of change

Sometimes the reasons for a difficulty in making or maintaining a change are not immediately obvious. The following exercise will help you to look at a problem in more depth. This method may not always help you to find the best solution but it will give you plenty to think about.

First identify the problem that you want to explore and write it down under the heading A1. It may be a decision you need to make or something you would like to change about yourself but which you are finding hard to do.

Find the opposite of this and write it down under A2. So, for example, you might write 'stay in this job' under A1 and 'actively look for another job' under A2 or 'smoker' under A1 (something you would like to change about yourself) and 'non-smoker' under A2.

Write down the disadvantages of A1. Think of as many as possible.

Now list the advantages of A2.

You can now begin to look at the reasons why it might be difficult to change. Begin by finding the ADVANTAGES of A1 (your present situation). This highlights the 'payoffs' of staying as you are. Under A2 write down the DISADVANTAGES of changing.

Now look at the whole table and ask yourself (a) Do I still want to make the change? (b) If I still want to change is there any way of achieving it without losing some of the advantages I am experiencing at the moment? Is there a way in which I can reach a compromise? How can I resolve any dilemmas that this has shown up?

When you have completed this exercise you may have a better indication of why it is difficult to make certain changes. Perhaps it has given you some ideas of areas you would like to look at in more depth.

A1	A2
Disadvantages	Advantages
Advantages	Disadvantages

5.11 Summary

What I understand about the process of change:

What I understand about my own ways of coping with change:

My positive intention is:

So, you have thought about change and perhaps you are making decisions about the direction in which you want to change. You have thought a little about how you are going to begin to make these changes. This might be a good point to remind yourself that you are already a valuable, worthwhile person and that you are making these changes for yourself, not for anyone else. The need to be accepting of yourself and to recognize how much you are achieving along each step of the way is essential as you continue to progress.

Section 6

Self-Acceptance

Aims of this section

- to explore how our thoughts affect the way we feel and act

- to identify unhelpful patterns of thinking

- to appreciate skills and helpful beliefs

Information and activity sheets
INFORMATION SHEET 6A: THE VICIOUS CYCLE (PAGE 149)

Demonstrate this with a 'negative' thought identified by the group.

6.1 CHALLENGING YOUR BELIEFS (PAGE 150)

Beliefs that lower self-esteem might be such things as 'it's a family pattern', 'it's all down to fate', 'I can't make small talk', 'I'm the only person I know who can't do this'.

Beliefs that raise self-esteem might be 'I am in control of my own destiny', 'my achievements are due to my hard work, not just luck', 'my opinions are worth listening to'.

One belief is entered in each part of the wheel. The wheel helps you to go where you want to go in life. Beliefs that lower self-esteem cause the wheel to buckle or throw it off balance so you don't get where you want.

This image could be extended into talking about what tools are needed if a 'lowering' thought has buckled the wheel slightly. Perhaps some people can cope with a slight buckling and still get where they want, but at a slower pace. Maybe some repairs need to be made; perhaps some spokes need to be replaced completely. If the wheel keeps taking you off course what needs to be done?

6.2 SOME COMMON PATTERNS OF SELF-TALK THAT LOWER SELF-ESTEEM (PAGE 151)

Having looked at beliefs, participants are now asked to identify any specific 'self-talk' phrases that they use. In many instances of course we may not confine these patterns to internal dialogues; we may tell other people these things as though they were indisputable facts! One teenage group I worked with likened positive thoughts to healthy eating and unhelpful thoughts to eating 'junk' food. They managed to take this metaphor to its limit, describing the gruesome effects that too much junk food/junk thinking might have on your body! The fact that they had come up with the mind/body link on their own proved to be very effective in enabling them to see the relevance of positive self-talk.

Self-talk patterns	Examples
I know what you think (otherwise known as mind-reading!)	You obviously think I don't know what I'm doing.
Total disaster (catastrophizing the difficulty)	My whole world will fall apart if I don't know anyone at the party.
These things always go together	If I book a holiday something is bound to go wrong – it always does.
Everyone and always (overgeneralizing)	Everyone always thinks I'm stupid.
Compared to you	I can never match up to what anyone else can do.
I should (it is an unwritten law)	I will feel guilty/will somehow be punished if I don't do this/feel this.
I must	I don't have any choices. This is the only option.
The whole of me	I am so useless – my boss didn't even say good morning to me.
The world says	Everyone knows that…
	Everyone is saying that…
I blame the cat	My father/teacher/neighbour makes me feel inferior.
Vaguely speaking	It's all down to fate. People say strange things.

Once unhelpful self-talk patterns have been identified, individuals can be encouraged to confront them or challenge them, by making them much more specific. For example:

Group member: Everyone thinks I'm useless.

Facilitator: Who exactly thinks that you are useless?/What do you mean by 'useless?'

Group member: Teachers...the maths teacher/I can't do any of the homework.

Facilitator: Your maths teacher thinks you're useless at maths because you have found some of the homework difficult? How do you know that he/she thinks this?

6.3 ANALYSIS OF A DIFFICULT SITUATION (PAGE 152)

The following is an example of analysing a difficult situation:

My difficult situation is: I have to drive on my own to a meeting.

My usual thoughts are:	**How this affects me emotionally:**
I might get lost. I'll be late and everyone will think I'm stupid.	I feel anxious long before the time I have to go.
I can change these to:	**Emotionally I will feel:**
I'll plan my route the day before. I've got my mobile. If I'm late I'll be able to explain.	more confident because I will have planned what to do.
How this affects me physically:	**How this affects my behaviour:**
I get tense. I can't concentrate properly. I end up with a headache.	I don't get what I should out of the meeting because I'm so wound up. I end up being short tempered with people when I get home.
Physically I will feel:	**How this will affect my behaviour:**
more relaxed, more able to concentrate.	I will enjoy the meeting more. I'll listen to some music on the way back home and arrive back feeling more calm.

6.4 APPRECIATION (PAGE 153)

It may be difficult for some people to appreciate the skills they have or to see the relevance of these skills in different areas of their lives.

In order to complete the jigsaw, each person thinks of at least three things that they enjoy doing. They then think about what 'skill', quality or personality trait (asset) they have that enables them to enjoy this pastime. Each 'asset' is entered in the jigsaw. Discuss how many of these assets could be used when tackling a problem in a different area of life.

Marek enjoys football. In his jigsaw he wrote: co-ordination, agility, team player, determination, dedication, fitness, quick to learn, strategist, risk taker, not afraid to get hurt. During the group discussion he quickly came to see how he could transfer some of these assets to working on his difficulty with his speech.

Finish the exercise by encouraging participants to appreciate their greatest achievements. Emphasize that these are personal achievements, not achievements compared to anyone else. It may be an achievement for someone to enter a room full of strangers on their own and manage to stay for ten minutes.

6.5 WORK IN PROGRESS (PAGE 154)

This is a reminder that we don't need to have completed a task before we can start to feel better about ourselves. This also highlights the point that awareness of difficulties doesn't have to be an opportunity to give ourselves even more of a hard time – that there will always be things that we will be working on to some degree.

6.6 SUMMARY (PAGE 155)

See the notes for summary sheet in Section 2 (page 78).

Section 6
Self-Acceptance

The Vicious Cycle

What we believe to be true about ourselves affects the way we think. This affects how we feel emotionally, and this in turn has an effect on our physical state and therefore our behaviour. The cycle can be positive or negative. Here's how it might work:

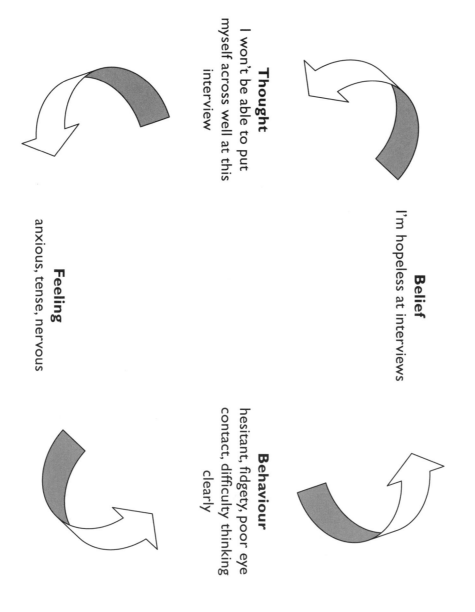

Belief
I'm hopeless at interviews

Thought
I won't be able to put myself across well at this interview

Behaviour
hesitant, fidgety, poor eye contact, difficulty thinking clearly

Feeling
anxious, tense, nervous

When things don't go well we can end up feeling bad about ourselves in a way that spills over into other areas of life. We might start to think 'I can't do anything well' or 'everyone else is more confident/clever/better looking than me'. Even when new evidence presents itself that would seem to contradict our belief we deny it or make it out to be unimportant, a 'one-off' a 'chance event', 'not of our doing', etc.

6.1 Challenging your beliefs

What are some of your beliefs about yourself and your life? Which of these strengthen your self-esteem? Which beliefs lower your self-esteem? How efficient is your wheel?

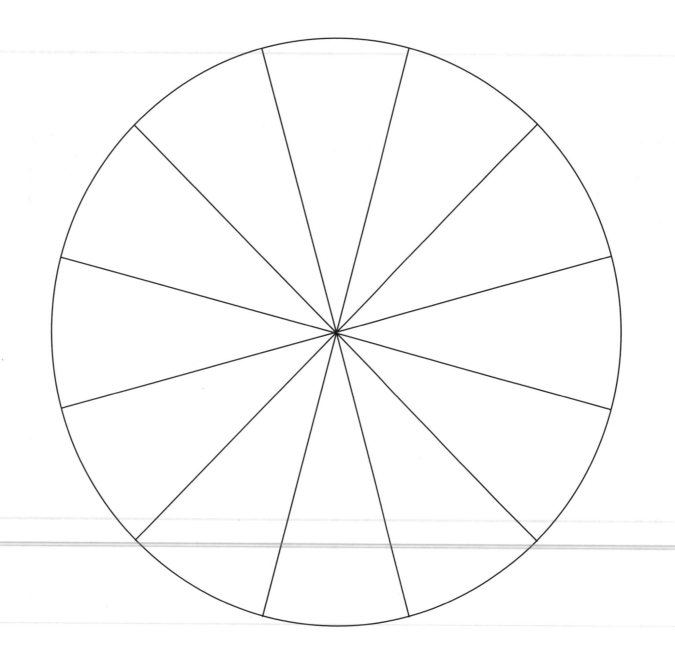

I know what you think

Everyone and always

The whole of me

I blame the cat

These things always go together

Compared to you

I should/I must

The world says

Vaguely speaking

Total disaster

Can you think of any others?

6.3 Analysis of a difficult situation

My difficult situation is _____

My usual thoughts are:

I can change these to:

How this affects me emotionally:

Emotionally I will feel:

How this affects me physically:

Physically I will feel:

How this affects my behaviour:

How this will affect my behaviour:

6.4 Appreciation

What would you most like other people to know about you? What do you appreciate about yourself? What are your skills and assets?

Complete the 'asset jigsaw':

What are your three greatest achievements in life?

6.5 Work in progress

What are you 'working on' at the moment that you are particularly pleased about or proud of? What would you like other people to praise you for attempting?

Write your list of work in progress.

6.6 Summary

What I understand about self-acceptance:

What I understand about my patterns of thinking:

My positive intention is:

Self-acceptance is, of course, the foundation for secure and fulfilling relationships with others. This is the next area to consider as you build your self-esteem.

Section 7

Self and Others

Aims of this section

- to reflect on how low self-esteem can affect how we behave in relationships

- to think about the importance of mutuality and individual rights within relationships

- to explore issues of assertive and non-assertive communication

Information and activity sheets

INFORMATION SHEET 7A: SELF-ESTEEM WITHIN A RELATIONSHIP (PAGE 164)

Use this for discussion in the whole group. Devise a possible 'vicious cycle' together, using an example offered by a group member if possible.

Although every relationship will have its difficulties, this may be hard to accept for those who have idealized views of friendships and intimate relationships. A 'healthy' relationship might be defined as one where each person has a secure, defined sense of self and is therefore able to let the other person be separate, rather than one looking to the other to fulfil their needs. A person with healthy self-esteem is able to be more aware of the feelings of others and to understand the importance of mutuality, striking a healthy balance between connectedness and personal autonomy.

Charles Tart makes a clear distinction between consideration of others shown through conditioning or 'habit' and the ability to 'see more accurately and discriminatingly and so behave more appropriately toward others and toward our inner selves' (Tart 1994, page 6). Tart refers to this type of mindfulness within relationships (including the relationship with ourselves) as a form of perceptual intelligence, rather like emotional intelligence. This is appealing because it suggests that we can develop and enhance the appropriate skills needed.

7.1 GETTING A BROADER PERSPECTIVE (PAGE 165)

At the point of imagining a conversation with the friend, encourage participants to actually move into another seat when they are 'being' that person. This activity is also a useful starting point for a discussion about empathy. For example, you might explore the difference between empathy and sympathy (see Part I, Chapter 5, 'Working with Groups', page 43).

I first experienced this exercise during a counselling skills workshop. We each had to think of a teenager with whom we were finding some difficulty. When we stepped into the shoes of the teenagers the atmosphere around the room changed very noticeably as people tried to feel what it must be like to be their teenage sons, daughters or clients! We gained some valuable insights that day and several of us later reported changes in how we handled the situation that we had been exploring.

7.2 SOME QUESTIONS FOR DISCUSSION (PAGE 166)

The discussion could be based on a specific type of relationship, such as with a partner or with a close friend, or be more broadly based to include several different levels of relationship. If numbers permit, divide up the group so that different groups discuss a selection of the suggested questions. Draw together the responses in the large group.

7.3 THE HOUSE OF RELATIONSHIPS (PAGES 167–8)

The house of relationships is adapted from an exercise on health and illness by Dina Glouberman (2003, pages 226–7). You could either lead this exercise with the whole group, demonstrate with one person so that participants can then facilitate each other, or, if you feel that a group member is ready and able, you could support him in facilitating the exercise for everyone else. The wording can also be made more specific. You might, for example, look for the expert on assertiveness rather than the expert on relationships. As before, whichever method you decide on, you will need plenty of time after the Imagework to talk it through with the whole group and to ensure that everyone is feeling OK with the 'advice' that they got from their 'expert'.

'R' explored her image of an assertiveness expert in her house of relationships. She found that her expert was a disliked teacher from her childhood, who appeared to be aggressive, rather than assertive. At first she found it very difficult to relate to this image. She rejected it and wanted to search for an alternative image in the house. However, when encouraged to stay with her original image and to step into 'being' the teacher she realized that one of the barriers to her own expression of assertiveness was the fear that people would react to her as she had reacted to this teacher – with strong dislike, even though she was fully aware of the difference between assertiveness and aggression. She gained valuable insights from this 'inner teacher' – an expert in how not to do it! (Plummer 2013, page 354)

INFORMATION SHEET 7B: WHAT IS ASSERTIVENESS? (PAGE 169)

Because issues of self-esteem are so multifaceted, I strongly believe that assertiveness training should not be undertaken in isolation, as if it were a 'method' for building self-esteem all of its own. This is one of the reasons why I have included it as part of an overall section on self-esteem within relationships. It could as easily have been placed in several of the other sections and this is worth pointing out to groups.

Assertiveness guidelines help us to take a problem-solving approach to life's challenges. I don't generally refer to assertive communication as using 'techniques' and I have tried to emphasize this on the relevant sheets. These are guidelines to support individuals while they establish for themselves what it is to enjoy open and honest communication with others.

I have included brief definitions of non-assertive behaviour here as these are widely known in the context of assertiveness training. However, I have also found Virginia Satir's outline of different communication patterns very helpful as a discussion point in groups (see the next activity sheet). You might find it useful to explore the links between these two approaches with your group.

Suggested reading

Dickson, A. (2012) *A Woman in Your Own Right: Assertiveness and You* (30th Anniversary edition). London: Quartet Books.

Holland, S. and Ward, C. (1990) *Assertiveness: A Practical Approach.* London: Speechmark Publishing Limited.

Satir, V. (1991) *Peoplemaking.* London: Souvenir Press.

7.4 THE CHOCOLATE DEBATE (PAGE 170)

(I am grateful to Marsha Lomond, a psychotherapist and fellow Imagework practitioner, who taught me the chocolate debate exercise in the context of a different set of roles.)

Family therapist, Virginia Satir, identified four common communication patterns when self-esteem is threatened:

Whenever there was any stress, over and over again I observed four ways people had of handling it. These four patterns occurred only when one was reacting to stress *and at the same time* felt his self-esteem was involved.

(Satir 1991, page 59)

The four patterns of communication are: *placating, blaming, computing* and *distracting*. All these are non-assertive communication patterns.

Divide the group into fours. Any extras should act as observers throughout the whole exercise. Explain that each person will have the chance to play all four roles and that these roles are to be played 'to the extreme'. Satir, in fact, includes descriptions of posture and voice quality but I have found that for this exercise participants quickly get into role and play the parts quite naturally. Explain the roles as follows:

- *Placater* – doesn't want to 'rock the boat' or upset anyone in any way so will tend to agree with everything (even when criticized) and try to make everyone happy. Takes the blame for everything, apologizes frequently, feels worthless.

- *Blamer* – finds fault with everything and blames everyone else for whatever goes wrong. Will use words like 'why do you always...', and 'you never do...' The blamer is aiming to appear 'strong' when actually they are feeling low in self-worth.

- *Computer* – cool, calm and collected. Tends to use long words in order to sound as though she really knows what she is talking about. Will often refer to something she has read on the subject. Appears 'without emotion', quite detached and very still (no expressive hand gestures!).

- *Distracter* – whatever the distracter does or says is irrelevant to whatever else is going on because he feels out of place. He is constantly moving around and fidgeting. He asks questions or makes comments that have nothing to do with the topic being discussed.

The group are to imagine that they are having a family discussion about chocolate. Actual position in the family (mother, father, child, aunt, etc.) is not relevant here. Each group sits in a circle. Everyone has just one minute in each role. At the end of the minute everyone moves round one chair to the left and assumes the next role. (If you have several groups doing this it can get quite loud and I have had to resort to ringing a Tibetan bell at times to indicate the end of the minute!)

This is a high energy, fun activity but it can bring up all sorts of feelings and recognition of patterns in self and others. It is crucial to give everyone the chance to de-role at the end of the exercise. Participants can do this by swapping chairs again and talking about what they are going to do that evening or what they had for breakfast.

Make sure there is still plenty of time left in the session to talk about how people experienced this and to reinforce the idea that behaviour patterns are not written in stone!

Satir identifies a fifth communication pattern which she calls *levelling*. A leveller communicates openly and honestly and their body language matches what they are saying and thinking:

Of the five responses only the leveling one has any chance to heal ruptures, break impasses, or build bridges between people. And lest leveling seem too unrealistic to you, let me assure you that you can still placate if you choose, blame if you like, be on a head trip, or be distracting. The difference is you know what you are doing and are prepared to take the consequences for it. (Satir 1991, page 73)

7.5 BEING HEARD (PAGE 171)

This activity is for discussion in pairs. Allow about five minutes for each person to talk about why it is important for various people to hear what they have to say. You don't need to use this list of course – perhaps some members of the group will have already identified particular people that they feel they would like to be more assertive with. At the end of the five minutes the listener feeds back what they have heard: 'It is important that your MP hears what you have to say because....'.

7.6 ASSERTIVE REQUESTS (PAGE 172)

Decide what you would like the outcome to be, but be prepared to negotiate. Discuss skills of negotiation and compromise. When are these appropriate? When might they not be appropriate?

Think about your body language. How do we reflect assertiveness in our posture and movements? You could refer back to the chocolate debate and talk about the different postures and actions used in the four patterns of communication during that exercise. Encourage awareness of intonation patterns. This is a simple request not an accusation! Contrast an aggressive tone of voice with passive and assertive tones.

Use 'I' statements. Take responsibility for how you are feeling. Remind participants of the communication guidelines discussed at the start of the course.

Be clear about the separateness between you and others. This is a reminder that we can alter the way that we react to people. We don't need to feel stuck in certain ways of being, even if the other person remains unchanged.

Be specific in your requests and ask the other person to be specific too. This is worth practising in the group. Ask everyone to come up with an assertive request for three different situations. These requests should specify actions very clearly, for example, 'I would appreciate your help washing up the coffee mugs next Thursday evening after the meeting' (rather than 'You never bother to help clear up after the meeting').

Acknowledge the other person's point of view (empathize). For example, 'I can see that you thought I didn't mind doing the clearing up but I'd find it helpful if you did the coffee mugs while I'm clearing up the kitchen.'

Keep an eye on your common goals. 'We both want to keep the place tidy for other people.'

Stay with your statement. Avoid allowing your self-esteem to be 'hooked', 'I don't enjoy doing all the chores on a Thursday. I'd find it helpful if you did the coffee mugs.'

7.7 SAYING 'NO' (PAGE 173)

Invite the group (in pairs) to try out different ways of saying 'no' to an unreasonable request without being direct. Discuss how it felt to be on the receiving end of an indirect 'no'.

Identify several unreasonable requests that could be role played in the group. Encourage participants to try easy 'no's' first and to save the more difficult situations until they have had several successes with the easy ones.

7.8 COPING WITH CRITICISM (PAGE 174)

Again, people need to actually try this out in the group. Participants may have had recent experience of being criticized and could devise an assertive response and try it out in role play with one other person. Otherwise, you will need a few possible scenarios ready for people to try.

It is, of course, important not to sound challenging when asking for examples or further explanation: 'I'd find it helpful if you could give me some examples of what you mean.'

Discuss other strategies that participants have tried that they feel have worked for them.

7.9 GIVING FEEDBACK TO SOMEONE ELSE (PAGE 175)

Rather than providing the guidelines here, this is an opportunity for group members to come up with their own ideas based on the skills they have already identified and practised.

7.10 GIVING AND RECEIVING PRAISE AND COMPLIMENTS (PAGE 176)

Emphasize appropriateness and sincerity in giving praise and compliments. It is best to look at the other person in a relaxed way; be sincere; use 'I' statements and be specific.

7.11 SUMMARY (PAGE 177)

See notes for the summary sheet in Section 2 (page 78).

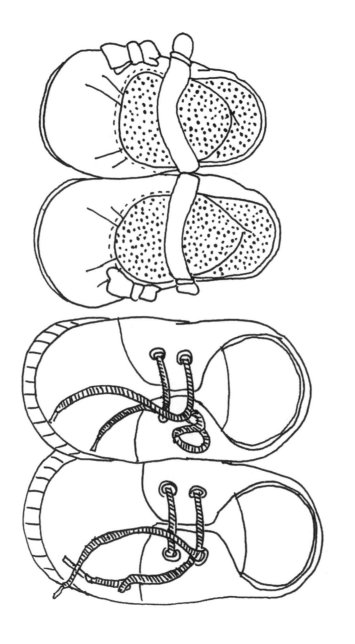

Self-Esteem within a Relationship

Levels of self-esteem have a big influence on how we form and maintain relationships with others. This includes important relationships with partners and close family and friends as well as with people we know less well such as people we work with for a short while or meet up with while we are at school or college.

How we see ourselves will affect how we view others. For example, if we think that people are judging us then we might act in a defensive way. This could mean that we become aggressive or perhaps very passive; or if we fear rejection we might be tempted to avoid forming close relationships all together. It is very likely that our behaviour will then affect how others behave towards us.

As with the 'vicious cycle' that we looked at earlier, this cycle of feelings and behaviours within relationships is not inevitable. When we feel good about ourselves we can handle difficulties much more successfully than when we are feeling low; we tend to trust others more and we are also more thoughtful about who we choose to have as our friends.

Although we can change our own thoughts and behaviour, we cannot force other people to change theirs. It might take time for people around you to adjust to the changes that you are making and for them to see you in a new light. You might find it helpful to talk about what is happening with the people who are closest to you. Tell them what you are feeling and how the changes you are making are affecting you.

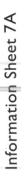

7.1 Getting a broader perspective

Think of a friendship you have had in the past that did not go as well as you would have liked, perhaps one that you felt had a negative effect on your self-esteem.

First of all think about what the other person did or said that you feel contributed to the situation not working.

Now think about what you did or said (or didn't do/didn't say) that may have contributed to the difficulty.

Imagine the person is sitting in front of you now. What would you like to say to them? What would you like to ask?

Imagine that you can become this person for a moment. As this other person, what is your perception of the situation? What do you want to say or ask?

Swap roles again and continue the conversation until you feel you have reached an understanding of some sort. What have you discovered?

7.2 Some questions for discussion

What do you think are the important elements of a secure, fulfilling relationship?

What do you feel are your 'rights' within any relationship?

What does the other person have the right to expect from you?

What are the special qualities that you are able to offer in a relationship?

7.3 The house of relationships

Imagine that you have the address for someone who is the world expert on relationships. You have the chance to visit this expert and ask any question about relationships that has been on your mind recently.

Take a few moments to imagine yourself finding this house. Just allow it to emerge in your mind… What does it look like?

Imagine yourself standing at the entrance and remind yourself of the question that you have come to ask… When you are ready, imagine yourself entering the house… Have a look around… What is the atmosphere of this house?… What are its qualities?… For example, is it new or old?… Does it feel busy or empty? What are your feelings now that you are here?

Somewhere in this house you will find the right expert to talk with. Have a look around until you find them… It could be someone you know, but it may not be! When you find the expert ask your question, talk with them about what is happening in your relationships…

Now imagine that you could become this expert for a moment… Step into being your expert. Take three full breaths as though you are really breathing into being this image… How do you feel?… What are your strengths?… What is your special quality or talent that means you are an expert on relationships?… What advice do you have to give?…

Continue the conversation, swapping between being 'self' and the expert until you feel that you have come to an understanding about your question… Finish as 'self'… Thank your expert and imagine yourself leaving the house… Gradually allow the images to fade from your mind and bring yourself back to the present moment…

7.3 The house of relationships (continued)

Make some notes or draw something that reflects your experience of meeting the expert.

What is Assertiveness?

Assertiveness is about believing in yourself and believing that your opinions and feelings are as valuable as anyone else's and that you have the right to express them. It is about self-respect and also respect for others. Assertiveness does not mean always getting what you want. It might sometimes mean negotiating or reaching a compromise.

Being assertive involves having enough self-esteem to be able to stand up for your rights without becoming aggressive.

It means being able to accept constructive criticism as well as cope with criticism that is not justified. It is recognition of the fact that you have the right to make mistakes.

Someone who is assertive is able to give praise freely to others without feeling that it somehow devalues their own achievements. They are also able to accept honest praise and not look for hidden motives or reject it as being false.

Assertiveness is about communicating clearly and confidently.

Non-assertive behaviour tends to be passive, aggressive or manipulative:

- Passive behaviour involves giving way to other people's needs, wants, opinions and feelings.

- Aggressive behaviour is about crossing other people's boundaries. This can involve such things as making decisions for other people as well as being verbally aggressive.

- Manipulative behaviour refers to actions that are aimed at trying to make someone else feel 'bad' about something or feel guilty.

These are types of *behaviour*, not types of people.

7.4 The chocolate debate

We all behave assertively sometimes but when our self-esteem is threatened there are some common behaviour patterns that you may be able to recognize in yourself or in others. Imagine that you and some other members of a fictitious family are having a discussion about the merits (or not!) of chocolate. You will each be given a different role to play in this discussion and you will get the chance to play all the roles. When you have finished, think about the following questions:

Which of the four ways of communicating was the easiest for you?

Which of the four was the hardest?

In your everyday life, which way of communicating do you tend to use when your self-esteem is low?

What have you learnt from this exercise? What decision can you make now?

7.5 Being heard

You may have had experiences in life that have led you to believe that your opinions and feelings are not important. If you feel this then now is the time to challenge that belief.

List five reasons why it would be important for each of the following people to hear what you have to say:

- Your partner/a good friend

- Your boss or someone else who has authority over you

- Someone you admire

- Your local MP

7.6 Assertive requests

There are certain strategies that can help you to remain focused and confident when you first start to experiment with assertiveness. Remember, these are only guidelines to help give you some structure.

- Decide what you would like the outcome to be but be prepared to negotiate.

- Think about your body language.

- Use 'I' statements. Take responsibility for how you are feeling.

- Be clear about the separateness between you and others. Just because someone says or does one thing doesn't mean that you have to react in a certain way.

- Be specific in your requests and ask the other person to be specific too.

- Acknowledge the other person's point of view (empathize).

- Keep an eye on your common goals.

- Stay with your statement. Avoid allowing your self-esteem to be 'hooked'.

7.7 Saying 'no'

Many people find it difficult to say 'no' to an unreasonable request without feeling guilty about it or worrying that they will lose the respect of the person who made the request. It is important to make it clear to yourself (and to the other person) that it's the request that's being rejected and not the person who made it.

If you have been asked to do something that you really don't want to do, how do you normally respond? Do you make excuses? Do you clearly state 'no'? Do you avoid making a decision? Do you end up complying with the request and feeling 'put on'?

Think about your experiences of either you or someone else saying 'no' in an indirect way.

Again, there are some simple guidelines to help in this sort of situation. When someone makes an unreasonable request:

- Notice your immediate physical reaction. This will give you an idea of whether or not you feel the request is really unreasonable (for example, you may experience a 'sinking' feeling).

- Give yourself plenty of time. If you notice yourself hesitating before replying then take this as a sign that you might need more information before you make a decision.

- If, after being given clear information about what the request involves, you still feel you need to say 'no' then try saying this clearly and simply without making lots of excuses. Remember to actually use the word 'no'!

- Make sure that your body language is also saying 'no' without looking overly apologetic or aggressive.

7.8 Coping with criticism

Listen carefully to what the person is saying. Do not interrupt with explanation or become defensive. Are you clear about the nature of the criticism? If not, ask for an example. Decide if the criticism is:

- completely valid
- partly valid
- not valid at all.

If it is valid:

- State what you agree with
- State how you feel
- Acknowledge the possible effect of your behaviour

  - 'Yes I was late'
  - 'I feel bad about keeping you waiting'
  - 'I realize this must have been frustrating for you'

If it is partly valid:

- Agree with the part that is true and disagree with the rest
- Say how you feel

  - You're right, I do find time-keeping difficult but I'm not lazy'
  - 'I'm offended that you think that'

If it is not valid at all:

- Reject it firmly
- Add a positive statement
- Ask for clarification

  - 'No. I don't agree. I'm not thoughtless'
  - 'I'm very enthusiastic about this project'
  - 'What makes you think I'm thoughtless?'

Finally, let it go! Don't automatically assume that a criticism means you have failed in some way. The other person is giving you feedback *from their point of view*. Look for consistent feedback from a number of people. Take responsibility for which aspects of the feedback you will act on; it is your choice whether or not to change your behaviour.

174

7.9 Giving feedback to someone else

Giving appropriate feedback to another person involves honest, non-judgemental information about how their behaviour affects you. Remembering the guidelines for assertive requests and assertive responses to criticism that you discussed before, what do you think would be appropriate guidelines for giving someone else feedback?

Guidelines	Examples

7.10 Giving and receiving praise and compliments

It is important for us to feel comfortable giving feedback to each other in the form of honest praise and compliments. This also involves being aware of 'filtering' of information. It is easy to reject compliments that have been given in all sincerity by responding with such things as 'Oh, it was nothing', 'I wouldn't be able to do it like that again' or 'I can't imagine why you think I look nice in this!' If we are able to accept genuine compliments and praise, as if we were accepting a gift, this will nourish our self-concept.

How do you praise/give compliments to others?

How do you feel when you are praised or complimented?

What is an assertive way of accepting praise?

How do you praise yourself?

7.11 Summary

What I understand about self-esteem within relationships:

What I understand about my own way of relating to others:

My positive intention is:

Even when we enjoy secure, fulfilling relationships with others it is important that we maintain responsibility for our own wellbeing. Do you respect yourself enough to take care of yourself and to ask for appropriate help when you need it? Have a look at the next set of activities. These may help you to decide whether or not you want to make changes in the way that you look after yourself.

Self-Reliance and Managing Stress

Aims of this section

- to help participants to identify any stress factors in their lives

- to identify personal reactions to stress

- to demonstrate the possibility of using positive self-help strategies to deal with stress

Information and activity sheets

INFORMATION SHEET 8A: STRESS MANAGEMENT (PAGE 185)

Use this for discussion in the whole group.

Levels of resilience to stress partly depend on our ability to moderate stress and on our coping strategies. These in turn will be influenced by personal temperament, environment, social support and past experiences. Understanding stress therefore involves understanding the unique relationship for each individual between their environment and their personal abilities and temperament.

One of the biggest stressors for any age group is the loss of (or fear of losing) a secure relationship. Some other common stressors include:

- school/work pressures, including exams and starting or changing schools/changing work circumstances

- unrealistic pressure for consistently high standards of behaviour and conformity to rules

- bullying, difficulty in making friends, ending friendships, making new friends, feeling 'different' from peers

- illness or physical disability

- persistent under-stimulation (boredom).

8.1 IDENTIFICATION (PAGE 186)

This could be a 'do at home' activity given out at the end of the last session on 'self-esteem in relationships'. Encourage individuals to look at such things as whether or not there is a particular area in which they experience a greater sense of stress than others. The same categories could also be used for listing possible coping strategies (see also activity sheet 8.3).

INFORMATION SHEET 8B: THE STRESS REACTION (PAGE 187)

Use this for discussion in the whole group.

8.2 PHYSICAL SIGNS (PAGE 188)

Encourage the group to share their experiences of stress and find common patterns. Particular emphasis should be placed on the connection between lowered self-esteem and stress reactions.

Neuro nugget

When stress is excessive or continuous over a long period of time, even at relatively low levels, we can experience a 'toxic' build up of stress hormones such as cortisol, which is released by the adrenal glands. Cortisol plays a part in raising blood glucose levels and in breaking down fat and other proteins to provide extra energy for the fight/flight reaction. However, high levels of cortisol can affect our memory capacity and will dampen our immune system. This, coupled with a fall in levels of dopamine and serotonin (feel-good hormones) in the pre-frontal cortex, can cause us to feel 'overwhelmed, fearful, and miserable, colouring our thoughts, feelings, and perceptions with a sense of threat or dread as if everything we need to do is far too hard' (Sunderland 2006, page 87).

The effects of continued stress at an early age can have far-reaching effects for our emotional wellbeing, making it more difficult for us to regulate our emotions in later life. This could result in over-reaction to minor stressors and being physically 'on edge', constantly on the look-out for possible dangers and problems. This hyper alertness is physically and emotionally exhausting and anyone in this state will naturally crave to re-establish a sense of normality and control in their lives. Unfortunately, some of the ways in which we choose to do this, either consciously or unconsciously, can also be detrimental to our wellbeing (see activity 8.3).

INFORMATION SHEET 8C: RECOGNIZING THE SIGNS OF STRESS (PAGE 189)

Again, the link between thoughts and physical responses (mind and body) can be emphasized. Some of these symptoms can obviously occur for medical reasons and may have nothing to do with stress. Participants need to be aware that we are simply looking at possible ways in which stress might affect us physically.

8.3 WHAT CAN YOU DO TO COPE WITH EVERYDAY STRESS? PAGE 190

Discuss this as a general topic in the group and then break into pairs or smaller groups to identify individual coping strategies. Listeners may be tempted to make suggestions as to what the other person should do in order to cope with different stressors. Pre-empt this by reminding everyone that what works for one person may not work for another and that the aim is to come up with their own solutions.

Coping strategies might be focused on dealing directly with the problem in some way (e.g. avoiding/walking away from a situation, taking physical exercise, talking it over with a good friend) or might involve changing the way we think about the problem ('This is quite exciting'), or learning to tolerate and accept it ('This is stressful but I can manage my stress levels well'). Coping techniques tend to be situation specific – what works for one stressor may not work for another. It can be useful to look at coping methods which do not work so well at this point. For example, increased alcohol intake or smoking might seem to (temporarily) relieve the feeling of stress for some people.

8.4 ENJOYMENT (PAGE 191)

Some possible reasons for enjoying a particular type of activity might be:

Involvement with others

Feeling relaxed

Feeling challenged

Being creative

Being in the open air

Improving fitness

Engaging the mind

Solving problems

Being quiet

'Letting off steam'

Discuss this briefly before splitting into smaller groups or pairs. Once individuals have had a chance to think about this, ask them to feedback to the whole group. Encourage everyone to come up with at least one thing that they will definitely do before the next meeting to bring more joy into their lives.

You could also incorporate an imagery exercise here such as 'Future me' (see activity sheet 2.2). Questions you could ask for the positive future are:

- What is your diet like?

- What do you do to maintain a healthy sleep pattern?

- What physical activity do you do?

- What form of relaxation do you use?

- How do you manage your time?

Share responses in the group after the exercise so that participants can pool useful strategies.

Spend some time planning a 'perfect day out'. See if there is anything from this that participants could actually do during the next week.

Neuro nugget

Enjoyable physical activity is a good way to relieve the effects of a build up of stress chemicals and to release feel-good chemicals into the body instead. Jogging, cycling, playing sport or just going for a walk can all be excellent ways to de-stress. Laughter is also known to have anti-stress effects, activating the brain's emotion-regulating centres and causing the release of opioids, the natural brain chemicals that induce feelings of pleasure and well-being (Sunderland 2006).

8.5 WORRY CRUNCHING (PAGE 192)

Brainstorm other effective 'worry crunchers'. Invite everyone to take one idea to try out before the next meeting. You could do this as a 'lucky dip' exercise. Write each type of worry cruncher on pieces of paper (it doesn't matter if you have to repeat some). Everyone takes one from 'the hat' and experiments with the idea during the coming week. If they really don't have any worries during the week then they could offer the idea to a friend or relative to try out or could spend some time asking others what they do to successfully deal with worries.

8.6 PROCRASTINATING AND PRIORITIZING (PAGE 193)

Suggested reading

Perry, A. (2002) *Isn't it About Time? How to Stop Putting Things Off and Get On With Your Life.* London: Worth Publishing Ltd.

8.7 POSTURE (PAGE 194)

Discuss this in pairs. Point out any common patterns in the whole group.

8.8 BREATHING PATTERNS (PAGE 195) AND INFORMATION SHEET 8D: INSPIRATION AND EXPIRATION (PAGE 196)

Use both of these for discussion in the whole group.

8.9 USING ABDOMINAL BREATHING FOR STRESS MANAGEMENT AND GENERAL WELLBEING (PAGE 197)

Based on a simple meditation technique, focusing on breathing can be effective in reducing feelings of stress, even for those who suffer from panic attacks. Although thinking about their breathing may be difficult at first, it is a very positive way of increasing awareness of what relaxed breathing feels like. Extending the time for doing this exercise from five minutes a day to ten also allows individuals the opportunity to experience the calmness of focusing on something other than worrying or distracting thoughts (see activity 4.1).

INFORMATION SHEETS 8E: RELAXING YOUR BODY (PAGE 198) AND 8F RELAXING EFFECTIVELY (PAGE 199)

You will find a selection of relaxation scripts in Appendix A (page 259).

Relaxation results in decreased metabolism and lower blood pressure and respiration rate. Research has shown that it also produces the subjective feelings of calmness and stability (Benson *et al.* 1975), so this is a really vital skill for all of us to master. Relaxation can be learnt and, as with any skill, regular practice is necessary so that it can become part of daily living.

Suggested reading

Kabat-Zinn, J. (1996) *Full Catastrophe Living: How to Cope with Stress, Pain and Illness Using Mindfulness Meditation.* London: Piatkus.

8.10 DIARY NOTES (PAGE 200) AND 8.11 RELAXATION SCORE SHEET (PAGE 201)

These can be used to encourage self-monitoring both during and after the course.

8.12 ACTION PLAN (PAGE 202)

Discuss goals in pairs or in the whole group to encourage people to be as specific as possible.

8.13 IMAGINE A MIRACLE (PAGE 203)

The miracle question is often used in solution-focused brief therapy (SFBT). The aim in SFBT is to help clients to create sensory-specific internal representations of what they want (as opposed to what they do not want). The question to the client might be something like:

Imagine tonight while you are asleep that a miracle happens and your hopes from coming here are fulfilled, but because you are asleep you don't realize that it has happened. What are you going to notice that is different about your life?

From an Imagework perspective the client is encouraged to imagine that they are experiencing the day as if it is *currently* happening, strengthening the experience by engaging with all the main senses: What are you doing now? What can you see? What can you hear? And so on. Alternatively, the person can imagine that they have reached the end of the day and they are looking back on what happened. Relevant questions might then be: What is the feeling that you have now? What did you do/not do to contribute to this feeling? What attitude got you here? What decisions did you make? (see activity sheets 2.2 and 11.5).

Another way of doing this is to allow an image to emerge that somehow represents 'you when your hopes have been realized'.

8.14 SUMMARY (PAGE 204)

See notes for the summary sheet in section 2 (page 78).

Section 8

Self-Reliance and Managing Stress

Stress Management

If you were going to enter a sports competition or go on a mountain trek you would need to be properly prepared and would take time to build your strength and stamina beforehand. Yet how often do you find yourself facing stressful situations in your life feeling unprepared, tired or simply unable to cope? When you look after yourself you are more ready to enjoy the exciting and fun things in life and more ready to cope with things that are challenging or difficult.

A certain amount of stress in our lives is useful and necessary. However, there seems to be a 'peak' of stress that each of us can handle – a maximum level of personal stress under which we can continue to function effectively. If our perceived stress goes beyond this level, or if stress is prolonged or managed inappropriately, it may become a problem.

The types of things that different people find stressful (their stressors) are very much dependent on personality and temperament. The way in which you react to your stressors and develop your coping strategies are also very personal.

Effective stress management therefore involves increasing your understanding and awareness of *what you find stressful*, *why you find it stressful* and your personal reactions to stress. You will then have more options open to you for changing aspects of your current stress management that are no longer helpful.

There are many ways of managing stress. As you work through the next few activities it is important to remember that we develop our coping strategies because we believe that they will help. Even some of the less beneficial ones often work for a short while. Don't be hard on yourself if you have chosen strategies that are no longer working. Ask yourself 'Why did I develop that particular strategy? What was my aim? Can I now fulfil that aim in a different way?'

8.1 Identification

Identifying and naming some of the things that you find stressful is an important first step.

Think of six or more situations that you find stressful. List them under the headings below. If you have more than one situation in any of the boxes try to put them in order of most stressful to least stressful.

Daily activity/work

Relationships

Health/physical wellbeing

Emotional wellbeing

The Stress Reaction

There are several ways in which too much stress can upset a person's wellbeing. There are also many normal reactions that occur when we are faced with a stressful situation. These reactions prepare the body for 'flight or fight', in other words to enable us to physically fight the oncoming threat or to run away from it. The fight/flight reaction includes the following signs:

- Your muscles tense for action. This can result in aches and pains or feeling 'shaky'.

- The heart pumps harder to get the blood to your arms and legs and your trunk muscles, ready for action. This can feel like palpitations.

- There is therefore less blood elsewhere and so your skin might go pale and the movements of your stomach may slow down or stop (giving you a sudden 'sinking feeling' in your stomach).

- Your salivary glands may dry up, causing a dry mouth or throat.

- Your breathing is likely to become faster because your lungs need to take in more oxygen more quickly and also get rid of carbon dioxide.

- You start to sweat because this stops your body from getting overheated.

8.2 Physical signs

We each tend to develop certain patterns of stress reaction, with some of the flight/fight responses being more pronounced than others. For example, some people respond to stress with raised blood pressure, others with increased intestinal activity, others with increased sweating, and so on.

All these very normal responses occur because the body is preparing to face or run away from potential danger. If the reaction is completed and the 'danger' is dealt with then the body can relax again. Unfortunately, we often produce this reaction in situations that don't actually need a physical response. These things might happen even when we are just worrying about something without resolving it, concerned about a forthcoming test, a potentially difficult conversation or being late for an important appointment. Unwanted stress reactions can also occur when the original stressful situation is no longer there but we have not done anything to ease the stress response.

What physical signs do you experience when you are under stress?

A threat to your self-esteem can sometimes have the same physical effects as if you were actually in some sort of danger and preparing to fight or run away.

Negative self-talk tends to prolong the stress response because if you tell yourself such things as 'I can't cope, it's all going wrong' your body continues to react by staying ready for action.

Recognizing the Signs of Stress

Some possible signs are:

- feeling tired/lethargic
- a change in sleeping patterns
- unable to 'switch off'
- feeling 'low'
- feeling frustrated
- feeling of tightness or a lump in the throat
- constipation/diarrhoea
- feeling anxious for no particular reason
- reluctance to go to school/work
- headaches
- indigestion
- an increase in reliance on alcohol, smoking or other drugs

- restlessness
- shortness of temper
- weepiness
- difficulty in concentrating
- changes in voice quality
- increase in hesitant speech
- difficulty in making decisions that didn't cause problems before
- increased susceptibility to anxiety
- persistent habits such as throat clearing or nail biting
- abdominal pain
- aching muscles
- change in appetite — eating more/less.

Some of these may occur for other reasons as well, but if you know they are stress related then appropriate stress management can help to alleviate these symptoms. Mark which responses you have experienced. Is there anything else you can think of that hasn't been listed?

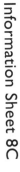

8.3 What can you do to cope with everyday stress?

Type of stress	What I can do

8.4 Enjoyment

Make a list of at least six leisure activities that you enjoy (even if you feel that you don't have enough time for them).

Think about what it is that attracts you to each of these activities.

Can any of the activities that you do at the moment be altered to include more of the elements that you enjoy? Are there any new activities you would like to get involved in which would include some of these?

Laughter is a great stress-buster! Researchers have found that when we laugh we release 'feel good' chemicals into our body. A good 'belly laugh' or 'a fit of the giggles' may even have effects on our immune system, helping us to fight some illnesses. Injecting some humour into our lives can provide an excellent boost to self-esteem.

What sorts of things make you laugh? How would you describe your sense of humour? How can you enjoy more laughter in your life?

Make a list of 'mini ways to look after myself'. This list might include such things as going for a short walk, going to the gym, relaxing in a deep bath or phoning a friend. Try to get at least twenty items on your list. Perhaps you could decide to do one of these things every day.

8.5 Worry crunching

Worry involves thinking about what we *don't* want to happen in life.

You will probably have been aware that during long periods of worry your body reacts as though the event is actually taking place now. Most noticeably, your muscles will tense ready for action. Worrying can wear us down and sometimes leave little room for other thoughts.

Writing a worry down or telling someone else often helps to ease it straight away. Make a list of the things that you are worried about at the moment. Be as precise as you can. Next, sort your worries into three categories: worries you can do something about, worries that you can't do anything about because they are not personal to you and worries that are from your past that you can forget about now.

Next to each of the worries that you can do something about write a short plan of action, for example, tell someone (specify who), be honest about saying 'no', make an appointment with the doctor, read up about it.

As soon as you make a decision to act you will find that the anxiety and tension will begin to lessen.

8.6 Procrastinating and prioritizing

If having too much to do is one of your stressors you may find it helpful to write down everything that needs to be done and put the items in order of priority.

Ask yourself 'What needs to be done today? What needs to be done by the end of this week? What could I ask someone else to do? What really doesn't need to be done at all?'

Prioritizing is not the same as procrastinating! Think about what happens when you put off doing something that you don't like doing. Perhaps it's a tricky phone call, or telling someone you can't help out, or finishing a piece of work. How do you feel if you keep putting it off? Some people prefer to do things at the 'last minute'. If you don't like doing this then making an action plan and getting started on it will take away a lot of the stress involved. This will free your mind and your time for something else that you do enjoy doing.

Things that I tend to put off doing:

8.7 Posture

Our posture and breathing patterns, like words and gestures, can be seen as ways in which we express our thoughts. When we are stressed we may show it in the way we sit, stand and walk. Our emotions can also be expressed at a more subtle level in our muscles. For example, someone who has always suppressed their tears may have a permanently tense jaw. Someone who is very angry or resentful much of the time may have constantly tense shoulders.

Identifying areas of unnecessary tension and learning how to relax the muscles can increase our sense of wellbeing and greatly reduce the stress reaction. An upright, balanced, relaxed posture can help you to feel calm and confident.

Draw a picture or body outline of yourself and mark any areas of pain or tension that you are aware of in your body:

8.8 Breathing patterns

A calm breathing pattern is another vital factor in the management of stress. It's very easy to take our breathing for granted because it's an automatic activity and most people don't think about it on a conscious level.

If you watch a baby or young child asleep you will see the ideal breathing pattern – slow, deep and regular. Their stomach will be rising and falling easily and smoothly. However, breathing patterns can change, sometimes for prolonged periods of time. Health problems are an obvious cause. Breathing patterns may also change as a reaction to stress.

Check your own breathing pattern. Sit in a comfortable chair or stand in front of a full length mirror. Place one hand lightly on your chest and the other hand on your stomach. Watch what happens as you take a full breath in and then release the air slowly.

- Which hand moved the most?

- Did your shoulders rise?

- Did your stomach move in or out?

- Did your posture change in any way?

If your breathing was relaxed you will have felt your stomach expanding as you breathed in and falling as you breathed out. This movement will have been very relaxed and gentle. There will have been only slight movement in your chest. Your shoulders will have hardly moved at all. Your posture will have remained balanced.

Inspiration and Expiration

Breathing in is called inspiration or inhalation. Breathing out is called expiration or exhalation.

Inspiration involves muscle power and the two major sets of muscles used are the diaphragm and the intercostals. The diaphragm is the large dome-shaped muscle under the lungs. It divides your chest from your abdomen. The intercostals are long, strap-like muscles between the ribs. When your diaphragm contracts it becomes flatter and, because it is attached to the lower edge of your rib cage, this causes your chest cavity to increase in size. Air is then automatically drawn in through your mouth or nose and into your lungs. The lower ribs (called floating ribs because they are not fixed to anything at the front of your body) move outwards as your lungs fill with air. The upper ribs are fixed to the breast bone and so there is not the flexibility for much expansion of the top of the lungs. The greatest area of expansion is therefore at the base of your lungs.

Expiration does not require muscle power. As you breathe out, your muscles simply relax and your lungs return to a smaller size ready for the next in-breath. This type of relaxed breathing is called diaphragm or abdominal breathing (although all breathing involves *some* diaphragm movement).

When you are physically tense or you are anxious you are more likely to use upper chest breathing. This type of breathing mainly involves the top half of your lungs. Upper chest breathing happens naturally as part of the stress reaction when we are under threat.

If you push air out you will be tensing your intercostal muscles and your diaphragm on the out breath. This type of forced expiration also involves muscles in the outer wall of the abdomen. These press upwards on to the bases of the lungs and force the lungs to become smaller so that air is forced out. All this extra tension increases the feelings of stress.

8.9 Using abdominal breathing for stress management and general wellbeing

As you can see, there is a very close relationship between breathing and relaxation. If your breathing is tense then your body cannot relax completely and if your body is tense then your breathing will not be as deep and regular as it could be. Abdominal breathing helps you to feel calm and focused.

Being aware of your breathing and training your mind to follow your breathing pattern (rather than be constantly preoccupied with other thoughts) for short periods each day can increase your feeling of general wellbeing and your ability to cope successfully with the stresses of daily life.

Getting started

Sit in a comfortable position, perhaps with your eyes closed so that you can focus completely on your breathing.

Start by simply being aware of your natural breathing pattern. If you are abdominal breathing already, then notice the rise and fall of your stomach. If you are upper chest breathing then remember that the idea is to relax your stomach as much as possible.

When you have established a comfortable rhythm to your breathing continue with the process for about five minutes. Your thoughts are bound to wander off onto other things. This is very natural. No matter how often this happens, just notice it and then gently bring your mind back to focusing on the rise and fall of your stomach.

Take time to do this every day for a week and notice any changes in how you feel when you are doing it.

Notice what happens if you take your attention to your breathing at various moments during each day. Notice what happens if you take time to establish awareness of abdominal breathing at times when you are feeling particularly stressed.

When you feel comfortable with five minutes of daily practice, begin to gradually lengthen the time that you sit quietly focusing on your breathing in this way. Aim to extend the time to ten minutes a day.

Relaxing Your Body

Our bodies need physical relaxation in order to balance out the times when we are using our muscles in physical activity. Relaxation also involves awareness and control of signs of stress.

You will have the chance to try out several methods of relaxation. Once you have chosen the method that feels right for you, you may find it helpful to record the instructions so that you can relax without the need to memorize them.

Your initial aims when practising relaxation might be the following:

- to learn what it feels like to be totally relaxed

- to discover any particular areas of tension in your body and to learn how to control these

- to experience a sense of control over any moments of anxiety in your life.

It is very important to keep practising. You may not experience immediate results; it may take a few weeks before you begin to feel the benefits in your daily life, but it's important that you continue to make time in your life for developing this skill.

Relaxing Effectively

There are certain conditions that will help you to relax more easily:

- You will need to set aside about 30 minutes during which you know you are unlikely to be interrupted. It is important that you don't feel constrained by the time limit or feel that you need to rush to do something else as soon as you've finished. Ideally this relaxation time should be at least once a day (twice if you feel you can manage it).

- Wear loose clothing and make sure that the room temperature feels comfortable.

- Choose a comfortable position, either lying down or sitting in a chair with good back support. If you are sitting and your feet don't easily reach the floor it's essential that you use some form of support so that you are not tensing your leg muscles.

- Don't worry about whether or not you are successful in achieving a deep level of relaxation. Just allow relaxation to occur at its own pace. Expect other thoughts. When you notice these distracting thoughts just let them pass through your mind and gently go back to focusing on your chosen relaxation method.

- Eventually you will notice the feelings of relaxation coming more and more easily.

- When you finish, sit quietly for a few minutes, at first with your eyes closed and then with your eyes open. The next thing that you do should be very calm and slow. Take your time, move gently and speak in a relaxed way so that you can keep the feeling of calmness and stability for as long as possible.

8.10 Diary notes

Note down those times when you think you will be able to spend time relaxing during the coming week. After each relaxation session make a note of how things went.

	a.m.	p.m.
Monday		
Tuesday		
Wednesday		
Thursday		
Friday		
Saturday		
Sunday		

8.11 Relaxation score sheet

Day	Time	Before	After

Give yourself a score of between 1 and 10 as to how tense you felt before and after each relaxation session. For example, a score of 1 would mean that you were very relaxed and a score of 10 would mean that you were very tense.

Do this for each type of relaxation that you try. This will help you to decide when it is the best time of day for you to practise and which type of relaxation technique is most suitable for you.

8.12 Action plan

Write down three things that you will do in order to achieve a greater degree of control in the management of stress during the next week. Be as specific as possible. For example, 'When I notice signs of stress I will go for a walk for 15 minutes; use diaphragm breathing; take some time for myself; talk to a friend.'

1.

2.

3.

8.13 Imagine a miracle

Imagine that while you are asleep tonight a miracle happens – any stresses that you are feeling at the moment completely disappear. You don't know that this miracle has happened because you are asleep but when you wake up in the morning you feel very different.

Imagine that it is actually tomorrow morning. Think yourself into being in bed, having just woken up. Take your time to really get a sense of yourself waking up and feeling stress free. What is the first thing you notice about the way you feel physically? How do you feel mentally? And emotionally? Imagine yourself opening your eyes. What can you see? What can you hear? How do you get out of bed? Do you get up slowly or do you leap up? How do you get ready for your day? What do you have for breakfast? What are you thinking about?

How do other people know that you feel different? What do they notice about the way that you look; about the expression on your face; about how you sound?

Do you notice anything different about other people? How do they greet you?

How do they look at you?

What do you imagine happening as you go through the morning? Keep asking yourself 'what am I doing/feeling/saying/thinking/experiencing that is different?' Try to fill in as much detail as possible.

When you feel that you have a real sense of how your morning unfolds when you are stress free, let the images fade from your mind and bring yourself back to the present moment.

Put down some thoughts about what you have just experienced.

Now here's the challenge. Is there anything you have written down that you could do tomorrow? What if you lived tomorrow morning *as if the miracle had happened?!*

8.14 Summary

What I understand about being self-reliant and the management of stress:

What I understand about my own management of stress:

My positive intention is:

When we start to manage our stress levels effectively we have more thinking space and energies left to develop other areas of our lives. The next section looks at how you can divert some of this energy into recognizing and developing your social skills and your unique way of expressing who you are.

Section 9

Self-Expression

Aims of this section

- to explore the main elements of successful social communication

- to allow participants the opportunity to devise some useful strategies for social interaction

- to continue to reinforce the mind/body link

Information and activity sheets

9.1 SOCIAL SKILLS (PAGE 211)

The main elements to encourage participants to think about are:

- understanding and using non-verbal communication successfully (including awareness of appropriate proximity to others)

- asking/answering questions

- active listening

- opening and closing a conversation

- making requests

- taking turns in conversation

- giving personal information

- explaining/giving instructions

- encouraging and reinforcing others

- giving and receiving praise/compliments (see also Activity 7.10, page 176)

- keeping an interaction going/staying on the subject
- applying appropriate problem-solving strategies in order to 'repair' interactions when needed
- being flexible in communication style (e.g. according to age of listener)
- being appropriate and timely in interactions.

In order to demonstrate these skills successfully we need certain abilities and qualities:

- imagination – an important element of empathy
- self-awareness and self-control
- adaptability
- tolerance and respect of differences
- an understanding of the 'mutuality' involved in successful communication.

Social competence is a 'dance' between all participants – with each person appraising and adjusting the nuances of interaction, often at an unconscious level. Those who do not learn to master this dance are often seen as insensitive or big-headed and may be quick to anger because they misread social signals. Their awkwardness and anxiety may cause others around them to feel anxious in their presence and their consequent negative social experiences may lead to chronic low self-esteem. Various studies have also demonstrated a link between childhood difficulties with social interaction and later problems in adulthood, such as persistent anxiety and depression. In extreme cases, inappropriate social interactions can lead to complete social rejection. As Daniel Goleman points out, people who fail to follow the unspoken rules of social harmony 'inevitably leave disturbance in their wake' (Goleman 1996, page 121).

Allied to these principles is the notion of self-efficacy (see page 13). A sense of self-efficacy allows individuals to make intelligent use of social skills to influence others. This adds important ethical aspects to the interpretation of social competence. We probably all know of someone who is skilled enough in social intercourse to be able to manipulate others for their own objectives. Where interactions occur in the spirit of mutuality however, then outcomes are likely to be beneficial to everyone concerned.

9.2 PYRAMIDING (PAGE 212)

This is based on an exercise from Personal Construct Therapy. Start by asking the group to think of someone they know who they consider to be socially skilled. Identify three or four examples of behaviour which indicate that this person is skilled. Take each of these in turn and identify even more specifically what the elements of this behaviour are, refining the behaviours into smaller and smaller units. At the end of the exercise you will have identified some specific behaviours which participants can choose to incorporate into their social interactions. It is hoped they will also have recognized many aspects that they are already doing. This is an example of a pyramid of communication skills from a speech and language therapy group:

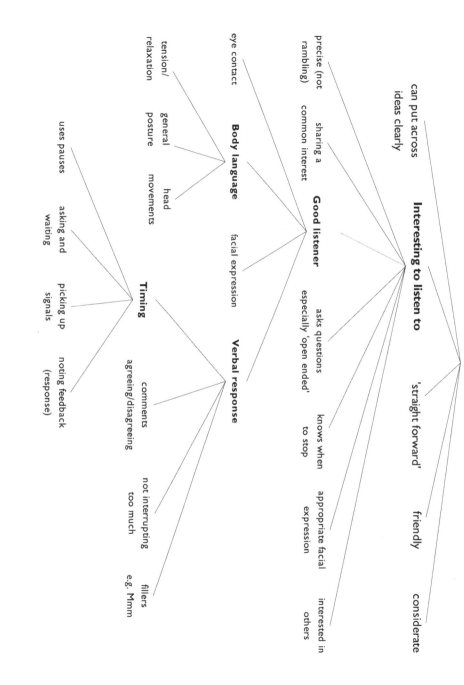

Successful Communication

- **Interesting to listen to**
  - 'straight forward'
  - friendly
  - considerate
- **Good listener**
  - sharing a common interest
  - asks questions especially 'open ended'
  - knows when to stop
  - appropriate facial expression
  - interested in others
- **Body language**
  - eye contact
  - facial expression
  - tension/ relaxation
  - general posture
  - head movements
- **Verbal response**
- **Timing**
  - uses pauses
  - asking and waiting
  - picking up signals
  - noting feedback (response)
  - comments agreeing/disagreeing
  - not interrupting too much
  - fillers e.g. Mmm

precise (not rambling)

can put across ideas clearly

9.3 EYE CONTACT (PAGE 213)

Use this activity for discussion in the whole group.

9.4 STARTING A CONVERSATION (PAGE 214)

Encourage the group to devise their own examples for each of the guidelines given on the activity sheet. For example:

Use open-ended rather than closed questions:

I heard you had a great holiday. What did you do?

Notice and respond to any new information:

Speaker: I thought I was going to be late. I'm not used to the buses here.

Listener: Are you new to the area?

Offer some information about yourself:

I sometimes use the bus too; I really enjoy not having to drive at weekends.

Brainstorm different ways that people initiate conversations. This is also a good 'do at home' task. Participants can be asked to observe precisely what friends and family (or characters from soap operas) do and say to initiate conversation, and then report back to the group.

9.5 LISTENING SKILLS (PAGE 215) AND 9.6 MAINTAINING RAPPORT (PAGE 216)

Effective listening skills include:

- maintaining focused concentration on what the other person is saying
- reflecting on what is heard
- showing interest by using appropriate facial expression and body language
- not interrupting
- not changing the topic
- asking appropriate questions to clarify if necessary
- keeping relaxed eye contact
- using natural prompts such as 'Mmm', 'Yes', 'I see'
- making links between different parts of what the speaker is talking about
- allowing more than brief silences to give the speaker time to think
- picking up on non-verbal cues to better understand what the speaker is feeling.

9.7 PAUSING (PAGE 217)

Why do we pause? Here are a few thoughts:

- to give ourselves time to think

- to give the other person time to absorb what we've said (we might also pause before answering a question in order to think carefully about what the other person has said)

- to take a breath

- because we are filled with emotion

- to emphasize a point

- to maintain a feeling of calmness.

9.8 ENDING A CONVERSATION (PAGE 218)

This could also be used for a 'do at home' observation task before discussion in the group.

9.9 BEYOND WORDS (PAGE 219)

This could be a useful time to revisit and perhaps rewrite or update the character sketch (see activity sheet 3.2).

You could also use a 'future self' exercise to strengthen the image of how each person would like to be seen (see activity sheet 2.2). My experience has been that many individuals have already started to make changes to their physical appearance by the time they are nearing the end of a course. Sometimes this is a very conscious choice, at other times the changes have seemingly been more unconscious.

9.10 IMAGINE IT AGAIN! (PAGE 220)

This task is aimed at further reinforcing the idea of state management (see activity sheet 4.3).

9.11 SUMMARY (PAGE 221)

See notes for the summary sheet in Section 2 (page 78).

Section 9

Self-Expression

9.1 Social skills

We learn some social skills from important adults when we are growing up and we develop some through interaction with our peers. Many work places also offer social skills courses as part of their training programmes. Using these skills in a more conscious way to support yourself in the changes that you are making can be very important in building and maintaining your self-esteem.

What do you think are the main skills involved in a successful social interaction?

Some skills may be useful in one situation but not in another. This will depend on such things as who you are talking with and the aims of the conversation.

9.2 Pyramiding

Think of someone you know who you believe is skilled in social conversation. Imagine that you are able to observe them at a party or having a meal with some friends. What is it that they are actually doing and saying that leads you to believe that they have good social skills? In the group you will be shown how to use a 'pyramid' structure to identify specific, concrete examples of socially skilled behaviour.

9.3 Eye contact

Maintaining appropriate eye contact is one indicator of feeling comfortable in a situation. When you feel your self-esteem is threatened you may find it difficult to keep relaxed eye contact with certain people. It may feel as though the other person can 'see' your true thoughts or recognize how ill at ease you are if you allow them to look directly into your eyes. However, if you do not maintain a natural gaze you are likely to give exactly the messages that you are trying to avoid!

Who do you think does more 'looking' – the speaker or the listener?

When you are speaking, what do you feel if the other person breaks eye contact with you?

When you are listening, what do you feel if the speaker doesn't look at you?

What signals do you give to other people if you maintain relaxed eye contact?

Is there any one person or any group of people that you find it particularly difficult to keep eye contact with? Do you know why? Would you like to change this? If the answer is yes, think of one very small 'experiment' that you could make that would help you to increase your use of this skill.

9.4 Starting a conversation

A key social skill is knowing how to start a conversation in a natural, relaxed way. Different people will have different ways of doing this and there really are no hard and fast rules, but once again there are some general guidelines which can help if you're feeling a bit hesitant about speaking with someone.

• Use open-ended rather than closed questions.

• Notice and respond to any new information.

• Offer some information about yourself.

Examples of open-ended questions:

Examples of noticing and responding to new information:

Examples of offering some information about yourself:

Do you or does anyone else in the group have other effective ways of starting a conversation?

9.5 Listening skills

If you watch good friends talking together you will perhaps notice a very natural 'rhythm' to their conversation. It is not uncommon for people who are on each other's wavelength to mirror each other's body movements. They will be talking at a similar volume and probably a similar speed. They are likely to be responding to what the other person is saying rather than introducing completely new topics. These are signs of being in rapport. Rapport is established through skilled 'active' listening but this can be surprisingly difficult if your own thoughts, feelings, questions and anxieties keep interfering. Such interference reduces the quality of listening and may lead to a breakdown in the communication.

What do you think are effective listening skills?

9.6 Maintaining rapport

For this next activity you will take turns with two other people to each talk about something that you are particularly interested in and that you think will interest your listeners. Each of you will have a turn at being speaker, listener and observer. When you are the listener use the 'active' listening skills that you have already identified. Your aim is to not just listen to the words but to try and understand what the speaker is thinking, feeling and meaning. The observer's task is to watch and listen and give feedback to the listener on which skills they have used. You can use the checklist that you made as a reminder. When you have discussed the exercise in your small group take some time to answer the following questions for yourself.

What elements of effective listening do you already use?

How do you show others that you are listening?

What percentage of a conversation would you normally listen for?

Are there any changes that you would like to make to your listening skills?

9.7 Pausing

You've already discussed the fact that effective communication is not just about speaking a lot, but most of us will have come across at least one person who, once they get started talking, doesn't seem to pause for breath! Pausing is important for a variety of reasons.

Why do we pause?

Do you think you use pauses appropriately? Are you able to tolerate silences within a conversation? Would you like to change anything about the way you use pauses?

How will you monitor any changes that you make?

9.8 Ending a conversation

What might be some of the difficulties involved in bringing a conversation to a close? Think about face-to-face interactions and mobile phone/telephone conversations.

If you want to finish a conversation but the other person sounds as if they could keep going for the next couple of hours what do you normally do or say? Is this effective?

How would you move on from one group to another when you are socializing with lots of people? Is this effective?

Do you or does anyone else in the group have ways of bringing a conversation to a close in a way that leaves everyone feeling OK about it?

9.9 Beyond words

Think about the clothes that you wear. What message do you give to others about the way you feel about yourself? Are you happy with this or is there anything you could change about your clothes and general 'style' to give a stronger message of 'I enjoy being me'? This doesn't need to involve a spending spree! It could be as simple as adding some colour, re-vamping some clothes that you had forgotten about or changing your hairstyle.

Write a manageable 'wish' list, draw some ideas or add some details to a new character sketch for yourself (see activity sheet 3.2).

9.10 Imagine it again!

Remember a time when you have been in a situation where you have spoken confidently and had an enjoyable conversation with someone. Imagine yourself being in that situation again.

- What do you sound like?
- What do you look like?
- What does your body feel like?
- What are you thinking?
- What can you see?

This is what happens when I am speaking confidently:

My breathing is

My posture is

My speech is

I feel

My thoughts during speech are

My thoughts after speaking are

9.11 Summary

What I understand about social skills:

_____

What I understand about the way that I express myself:

_____

My positive intention is:

_____

While you have been identifying areas for change you have also been trying out different methods for solving potential or actual problems. Seeing problems as opportunities for progress and development and being able to find creative solutions can be a tremendous boost to self-esteem. So, how creative are you? Are you ready to invest some time in exploring this aspect of your abilities?

Section 10

Creative Problem-Solving

Aims of this section

- to explore a variety of methods for problem-solving
- to encourage awareness of existing skills in problem-solving

Information and activity sheets
INFORMATION SHEET 10A: CREATIVE PROBLEM-SOLVING (PAGE 227)

Einstein was famously creative in the way he used images to experiment with ideas and to solve problems:

Leaps of imaginative ideas, which need not be at all logical to begin with seem to be essential to any new departure, in science as anywhere else... For instance, Einstein made one of his great leaps toward the theory of relativity when he was about sixteen and carried out one of his 'thought experiments'. This was to imagine himself as a particle of light traveling away from a planet at the speed of light, and then looking back at the planet thinking how it would appear. (Rayner 1993, pages 146–147)

10.1 HOW DO YOU NORMALLY SOLVE PROBLEMS? (PAGE 228)

Ask individuals to suggest real problems that they have faced or are currently facing. Choose one and brainstorm possible ways of solving this. For this activity you are not looking for specifics but rather for general *methods*. For example a group member might say 'I would talk to my boss about it.' The general method that could be drawn from this might be 'Discussion with others' or 'Sounding out my ideas with someone else.'

10.2 WHAT SKILLS ARE INVOLVED IN PROBLEM-SOLVING? (PAGE 229)

Can you tie a knot in a piece of string without letting go of either end? The trick is to cross your arms before picking up the string!

Can you draw a dot inside a circle without taking your pen off the paper? Fold the corner of the page. Draw a dot at the tip of the folded corner. Draw a line towards the fold and then start to draw a circle across the fold. Open up the paper without taking your pen off and complete the circle.

Ask group members to share similar activities or to find one to bring to the group next time. Another well-known problem of this sort is the problem of the nine dots:

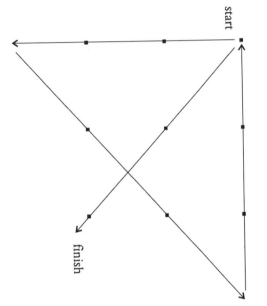

The task is to connect all the dots using four straight lines and without taking your pen off the paper. The solution is to extend the lines that you draw beyond the imaginary square that you first see in the pattern of dots.

This sort of task highlights the notion that for some problems we may need to look beyond our usual way of thinking and think 'outside the box'. I remember being shown this by one of my teachers – it can be very frustrating when you are trying to work it out and yet seems so obvious once you know how. But isn't that the way sometimes with some of our problems?!

10.3 PROBLEM FOCUSED OR SOLUTION FOCUSED? (PAGE 230)

This could be facilitated as an imagery exercise, by asking participants to imagine themselves as though they were actually in the situation again. In this instance, instead of projecting forward to a time when a problem has been solved you are inviting participants to recall a time when they've already used effective skills. They can then be encouraged to think about how any of these skills might be useful for tackling a current difficulty.

10.4 ANOTHER EXAMPLE (PAGE 231)

A quick search of the internet will bring up numerous ideas for problem-solving strategies. I used to offer ideas that I had personally tried but I have since found it more effective to encourage group members to do their own research, choose one method and try it out for a longstanding (but not major) problem. They can then report back on how things went at the next meeting. This activity sheet therefore simply offers one of the most well-known strategies as a starting point for further exploration. Alternating between focused concentration and 'engaging the mind effortlessly' is a key component in moments of inspiration. You might concentrate on solving a problem and get absolutely nowhere (or so you think!) then you go for a walk or soak in a bath or begin to drift into sleep and suddenly the answer comes.

10.5 USING IMAGERY (PAGE 232)

This is adapted from the 'Image as metaphor' exercise by Dina Glouberman (2003, pages 94–116). Once again, this could be a good opportunity for a group member to try out their facilitation skills with the whole group, or for participants to work in pairs. Whatever method you use, it will also be an opportunity to remind participants of the guidelines for giving honest praise and positive feedback to the facilitator(s).

10.6 USING DRAWING (PAGES 233–5)

Drawing can be used to explore situations and questions by people who usually rely heavily on words and logic just as easily as by those who cannot find the words to describe and explore difficulties as they would like. In a similar way to using visual images in our minds, drawing can also be used to look at different aspects of the same thing and to create links between present and future. This is an exercise I was shown at a workshop run by Tom Ravenette who used drawing extensively in his work as an educational psychologist. 'A drawing and its opposite' may reveal something about the artist that they had not thought of before.

Another way of doing this is to use two pieces of tracing paper. On the first piece draw an image that somehow represents the difficulty/problem/uncomfortable feeling. On the second piece draw an image that represents the opposite of this (or a preferred feeling). Put one picture on top of the other and see what emerges. People are often able to pick out an aspect of the combined drawing that will help them to get closer to understanding and dealing with their dilemma or problem situation. If there is no obvious indication of this the person can be encouraged to just hold the pictures in mind for the next day or two. As with the miracle question (see activity sheet 8.13) simply identifying the preferred situation or feeling will help the person to focus on their goal and will often trigger changes in thinking and in behaviour.

10.7 SUMMARY (PAGE 236)

See notes for the summary sheet in Section 2 (page 78).

Creative Problem-Solving

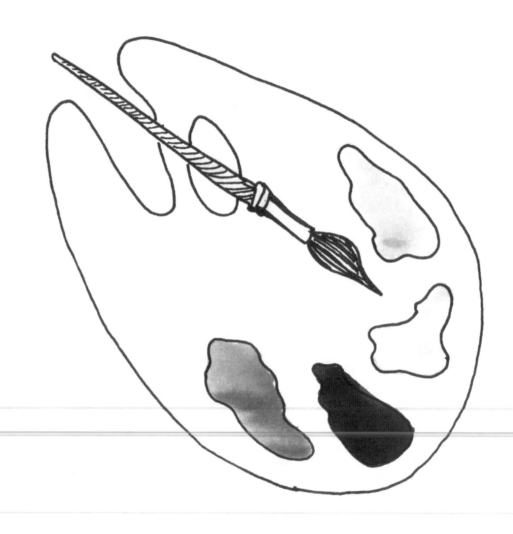

Creative Problem-Solving

The same method of problem-solving may not necessarily work for different situations and different types of problem. This is why it is important to develop creativity in dealing with difficulties.

Do you tend to be quite logical and methodical? Do you use intuitive ideas? Each time you solve a problem in a new way you are developing your creative potential. This can be effective even in times of extreme difficulties. If we believe that we are capable of finding a way through even seemingly insurmountable problems then we are much more likely to be experimental in dealing with difficulties. As we experience successes we start to trust our judgements and decisions more and more. This helps to confirm our abilities and self-worth and gives us confidence to know that we will be able to cope with future difficulties effectively.

Take some time to think how you normally go about problem-solving. In your group you will discuss a range of difficulties that might require different approaches. Write down some ways in which you would start to generate ideas about these difficulties.

In this exercise you are not looking at the ideas themselves but just at methods of coming up with creative solutions. For example, do you normally write lists of pros and cons for different ideas? Do you have 'brainstorming' sessions with other people? Do you meditate? There is no right or wrong answer, just see what you can come up with.

10.1 How do you normally solve problems?

a)

b)

c)

d)

e)

10.2 What skills are involved in problem-solving?

See if you can 'solve' these problems:

- Can you tie a knot in a piece of string without letting go of either end?
- Can you draw a dot inside a circle without taking your pen off the paper?

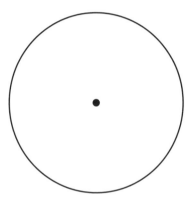

When you have worked out how to do these two tasks, take some time to think about the skills that you needed in order to 'solve' the problems. Can any of these skills be used to help solve other problems?

10.3 Problem focused or solution focused?

Problem-solving is about focusing on possible solutions rather than dwelling on the problem itself. Perhaps there has been a time recently when you have solved or reduced a problem. What did you do? How did you arrive at a solution? What steps did you take? Be as precise as possible in recalling the details of this. Think about your thought processes, your feelings and your actions. What worked? What didn't work? What did you learn from the experience?

The problem was:

I felt:

The way I thought about it was:

My decision was:

My first step was:

Then I:

The outcome was:

I felt:

What I learnt from the experience:

10.4 Another example

If you feel 'stuck' while working on a problem try putting your energies into something physical such as going for a walk or a cycle ride. You may find that a solution comes to mind when you are least expecting it.

What other methods of creative problem-solving appeal to you? Look on the internet; ask family, friends and colleagues; carry out some research at your local library. Choose one method and resolve to try it out during the next few days so that you can report back to the group on how it went.

10.5 Using imagery
(Based on an exercise by Dina Glouberman)

Think of a difficulty that you are currently working on. Sit quietly for a few minutes and let yourself gradually relax. Allow your eyes to gently close.

Invite an image to come into your mind that represents the difficulty. It might be an image of an animal, an object or a plant. Just allow whatever comes to mind no matter how strange or ordinary it might seem.

Now examine the image very closely. Look at where it is, notice its relationship to its environment. Is it alone or are there other things around it? How does it look from all angles; from in front and behind, from above and below? Does this image move or make sounds? If it could talk, what would it want to say to you? Find out as much as you can about this image, remembering that it represents your present difficulty. What is its history? Has it always been like this or was there a time when it was different?

Now imagine that it is some time in the future and that your difficulty has been resolved. How does your first image alter? Do not force it to change, just let things happen. Again, look at its environment, examine it from all angles. Is there anything there that you hadn't noticed before? What is the next step for this image? Where would it most like to be? If it needs to change any more, how will it change? Imagine this change taking place as you watch.

When you are ready allow the image to fade and gradually become more aware of your present surroundings. Take your time over this and as you become more alert remain sitting quietly and see if you can 'map' your image onto your actual difficulty. How does the image relate to possible solutions? How do the alterations in your image relate to the problem to be solved? Sometimes the answer is clear, sometimes you will need to bring the image to mind over a period of days to make sense of it.

10.6 Using drawing
(Adapted from an exercise devised by Tom Ravenette)

In a similar way to using visual images in our minds, drawing can also be used to look at different aspects of a problem and to create links between present and future. Using drawing as a method of problem-solving may give you added insight to a situation.

Sit quietly for a moment and choose a difficulty that you are working on. When you have chosen something just let it sit in your mind – don't try to consciously work out a solution. Using the line below as a starting point, draw a picture that fills the rest of the page. Don't think too deeply about it and don't worry about 'getting it right', just allow the drawing to emerge. Remember, fill the whole space; don't restrict yourself to one object but think about the background as well.

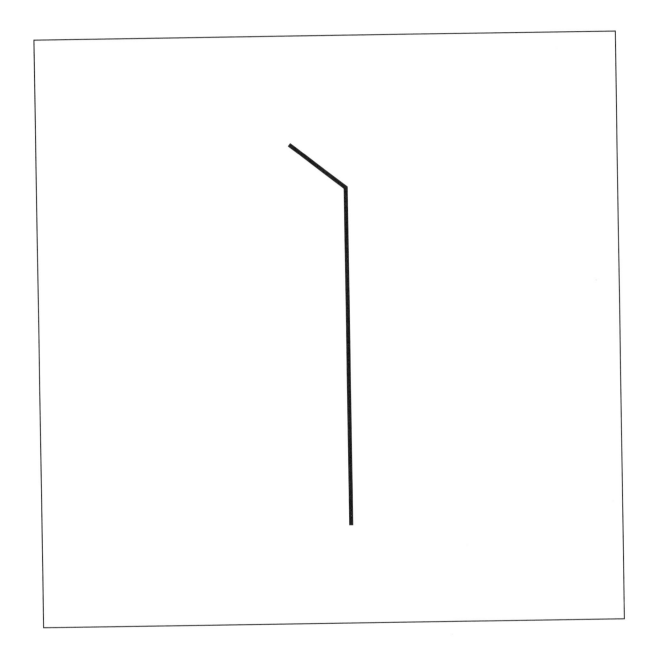

10.6 Using drawing (continued)

When you are satisfied that your drawing is complete, look at it carefully and then draw a second picture which in some way represents the opposite of the first.

Now look at these two pictures side by side and see how they represent your dilemma/difficulty/concerns. What associations do you have with the two images you have drawn?

Now draw a third picture. Draw anything you want to, the first thing that comes to mind.

If this third picture represents three ways of solving your problem, what would they be?

10.6 Using drawing (continued)

Sometimes the solution to a difficulty does not involve an opposite extreme. For example, if I am feeling overwhelmed in a very demanding job I might feel that I would be happier in a job with little or no responsibility. However, it may be that the skill I need to cultivate is assertiveness so that I can say 'no' to unreasonable demands on my time and be ready to delegate tasks to other people. In the exercise you have just done, the third picture represents some creative alternatives for you to consider beyond that which may seem more obvious at first.

A second exercise involving drawing is to simply sit with your question in mind and begin to make marks on the paper. If you are normally right handed, try using your left hand for this. Use different colours and draw without an end product in mind. It need not look like any particular object but will in some way represent how you view the situation or how you are feeling. When you have finished give your picture a name. Now add something 'surprising' to your picture. Once again consider how this relates to your question and whether or not it gives you an indication of how you feel things might progress.

There will always be more than one solution to any problem. Creative thinking helps us to find the way forward that is most appropriate for our individual needs at the time. It enables us to have choices. Choice leads to a feeling of control and to higher self-esteem.

10.7 Summary

What I understand about creative problem-solving:

What I understand about my own methods of problem-solving:

My positive intention is:

As you are beginning to make more conscious choices and changes in your life, it will perhaps have become increasingly clear to you just how important it is to set regular, achievable goals for yourself. This doesn't necessarily come naturally to many people — it is another skill that can be developed through practice. The following section outlines some methods for deciding on and implementing your goals.

Section 11

Setting and Achieving Goals

Aims of this section

- to reflect again on some of the obstacles to making changes and setting goals, with emphasis on those that individuals have already overcome or are currently working on

- to explore some possible goals for the future

- to understand the importance of creating hierarchies

Information and activity sheets
INFORMATION SHEET 11A: SETTING AND ACHIEVING GOALS (PAGE 240)

It is useful to set ourselves a mixture of short-, medium- and long-term goals. Too many long-term goals may be disheartening if there are no short-term ones to keep us motivated.

11.1 IF I WASN'T WAITING (PAGE 241)

This is a potentially 'high energy' exercise that is an easy one to do in pairs. I have found it useful to set a strict time limit for this: two minutes each with two minutes immediately after each person's turn for the listener to reflect back some of the ideas (but reassure them that this is not a memory test!). Hearing someone else voice your goals can be very empowering. You might also encourage the listener to use the present tense when they give feedback (as with the intentions set at the end of each section): 'You are spending more time learning the guitar and you are going out with friends every Tuesday.'

11.2 GUIDING PRINCIPLES (PAGE 242)
See Part I, Chapter 2, 'Self-Esteem, Learning and the Process of Change'.

11.3 AN EXAMPLE OF USING IMAGERY FOR GOAL-SETTING (PAGE 243)

You could lead the whole group in this exercise or if there is anyone in the group who already feels confident enough to facilitate this they could try it at home first and then lead the group at the next session.

Leave plenty of time after the exercise to let people talk about their drawings. Remind the group that we cannot interpret anyone else's drawings for them.

11.4 TAKING STEPS (PAGE 244)

This is another way of building hierarchies. As it is quite a lengthy activity it is best demonstrated with one person before participants pair up to facilitate each other. I have also used chairs set out in a row to facilitate this exercise, or paper stepping stones on the floor to emphasize the process of 'working towards' or 'stepping towards' a goal.

As noted before, imagery can be used very effectively in goal-setting by providing an opportunity to project yourself forward in time in your imagination and see a positive outcome, experiencing it in as much detail as possible and, in effect, creating a memory of the event as if it had already happened. This forward projection allows you the chance to recognize where you are at the moment – how far along the road you have already come – and also to discover some of the things that you will need to know in order to achieve your goal. Perhaps other people will need to be involved and you can visualize how this might come about. You can also explore some of the things that might hinder you: things that you will have to overcome in order to achieve your goal.

11.5 BEING EFFECTIVE (PAGES 245–6)

Discuss the process with the group. When everyone has decided on a goal give plenty of time for them to facilitate each other in threes. The third person can offer reminders of the process if the person facilitating wants some extra support. This could again be quite lengthy. Allow at least 45–60 minutes so that all three people have a chance to work with their goal and to facilitate someone else.

11.6 SUMMARY (PAGE 247)

Make sure that everyone has time during the session to make notes on their summary sheet and to state their positive intention aloud in the group.

Setting and Achieving Goals

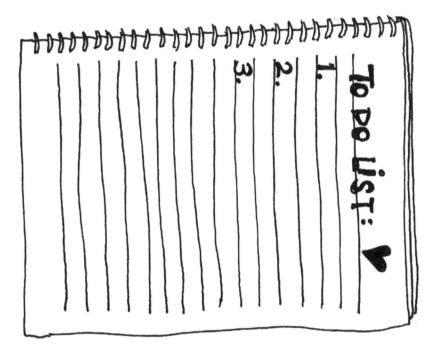

Setting and Achieving Goals

The ability to set realistic and yet challenging goals is an important skill. Like any other skill, it takes practice and dedication.

If you look back to the section on change you will remember that you discussed how difficult change can sometimes be and some of the reasons for this. Setting specific goals helps us to be in control of the direction of change and once again contributes to the maintenance of healthy self-esteem.

Fear of failure may prevent us from setting goals for ourselves on a regular basis. Sometimes we are told that we won't achieve our goals – 'that's just "pie in the sky"'; 'don't be silly – that won't work'; 'you'll never be tall enough/rich enough/ brave enough to do that'. If we hear this often enough then it may become our own self-limiting belief ('I never manage to do what I really want').

Sometimes we are encouraged to try out new things but we are unsuccessful because we have no real motivation to fulfil the goal or no clear idea of how achieving the goal would affect how we feel about ourselves.

Setting and achieving goals inevitably involves an element of risk – we risk making a mistake but we also risk success. Setting unrealistically high goals for ourselves may make the risks seem too huge and prevent us from taking the first steps.

For all these reasons it is important to take things one step at a time and, as we begin to make changes and achieve our goals, to give ourselves a 'pat on the back'. As young children we rely heavily on recognition and praise from the important people in our lives but as we get older it becomes increasingly important for us to recognize our own success and feel good about it. In this way we can build a stronger sense of self-worth.

So, each goal we set ourselves needs to be realistic and manageable. We need to be clear about what we are aiming for and when we want to have achieved it by. Each goal should fit in with our own beliefs about what is 'right' for us, and we need to recognize the benefits of achieving it.

11.1 If I wasn't waiting

Take two minutes to sit with one other person and complete the sentence 'If I wasn't waiting I would...' (wash the car, write a book, learn to swim, etc.) as many times as possible. This is a fast exercise. Don't think about it in too much depth. Some important things may occur to you during this exercise. Spend a few moments afterwards writing all or some of them down. Perhaps they will form the starting point for you to set yourself more regular goals.

Now ask yourself what exactly you are waiting for – more time, more money, more freedom, more confidence, more energy? Ask yourself if you really need to wait any longer for all the things you listed.

11.2 Guiding principles

The goals that we set for ourselves need to fit in with our view of ourselves and the world. We all have 'guiding principles' that inform our thoughts and actions. These are very central to who we are and we are and we are only likely to alter them if we have evidence that they are no longer valid or useful. What do you think are some of your guiding principles in life? You could think of these as 'unspoken rules' – things that you feel are 'taken as read'. These often involve words such as everyone, always, wrong, should and must. For example some 'rules' might be: 'It's wrong to show your emotions'; 'You should always think of others first', 'Everyone has the right to work'.

When you are deciding on your goals you may find it helpful to ask yourself 'If I achieved this would I really want it?' If you have any doubts then you have another choice: do you want to alter your goal or do you want to rethink any of your 'guiding principles' that may no longer be valid or useful?

11.3 An example of using imagery for goal-setting

Have a large sheet of paper and some coloured pencils near you.

Sit quietly for a few minutes and let yourself relax as fully as possible. Gradually close your eyes. Allow your imagination to come up with an image for the question: 'Where am I in my life right now?' This might be an image of an animal a plant or an object. Just allow whatever comes to mind.

Now, in your mind, examine the image very closely then when you are ready open your eyes and sketch the image on your piece of paper.

When you have finished sit quietly again with your eyes closed. Breathe deeply and relax. Allow an image to emerge for the question 'What is my next step?' Explore whatever image comes to you. When you are ready open your eyes and draw the image.

Repeat this process for the following two questions:

- What is getting in my way/holding me back?

- What quality do I need to develop in order to get me through this block?

When you have drawn the fourth picture take some time to think about how these images relate to your questions. You might find it helpful to talk to someone about what you have drawn in order to clarify what it all represents. Remember though that no one else can interpret your images for you. They are very personal and will trigger your own unique associations. Only you know what significance they have.

11.4 Taking steps

Some undertakings can seem huge when looked at as a whole, but when they are broken down into smaller steps they can become much more manageable.

Think of something that you would like to achieve in the next few weeks. State your intention as clearly as possible, for example, 'By the end of this month I will be going to the gym twice a week, every Monday and Thursday evening', or 'By Friday of next week I will have given a short talk about science fiction films to the youth group and it will have gone well'.

Imagine that there is a 'time line' on the floor in front of you. This line stretches from the present moment to the time when you have completed your chosen goal successfully.

Stand at the starting point of this imaginary line and take a few moments to get a sense of what you feel about this goal. What do you feel physically? Emotionally? Mentally?

Step off the line and look at the end point. Remind yourself of your positive intention.

Walk to the end point (without walking along the imaginary line!).

Stand at the end point of the line and imagine that you have successfully completed your goal. Take as much time as you need to really get a sense of how it is to have achieved your goal. What do you feel physically? Mentally? Emotionally?

When you feel ready, take a step back along the line to a time just before you completed the goal (it could be a few minutes or hours before, or the day before). What are you doing to prepare yourself for completing the goal? What are you feeling? What's happening around you? What are you particularly pleased about?

Now take another step back along the line to a point when something different is happening, perhaps a couple of days before completing the task. What are you doing? What are you feeling? Is anyone else helping you in this task? What are you pleased about? What is difficult? What is easy?

Continue back along the line, stopping at different stages and asking yourself these questions until you reach your starting point again.

Take a moment to look along the line and remind yourself what you learnt and what you experienced along the way.

Step off the line. Bring yourself fully back to the present moment by saying something about how you are feeling right now (calm, tired, excited, etc.) and how you know that you feel that way (my hands are tingling; my breathing is slow and so on).

Draw your time line and mark on it the different steps (smaller 'sub-goals') that led up to completion of your final goal. Remember that these sub-goals need to be flexible. Maybe you will find that you can miss out a stage or add an extra one or slightly change the order. Whatever you decide you will probably find that this exercise has helped you to see whether or not your goal is realistic and achievable within the time frame you have set yourself. Looking back as though it had already happened can be a great boost to your confidence. Making a note of the steps you took along the way can help as a reminder for future goals.

11.5 Being effective

Goals can be made for every area of our lives – at work, school or college, at home, within our family, amongst friends. They can be goals for things we want to achieve for ourselves or for others. We need to set ourselves a mixture of long-term, medium-term and short-term goals.

It's important to choose goals that feel 'right' for you. There are some simple questions you can ask yourself that will help you to choose effectively.

Remember the imagery exercise you did in the section 'What Is Self-Esteem?'

Here's a reminder:

Read through the following instructions or have someone read them to you. When you are ready, close your eyes and relax your body. Imagine that it is the end of the situation you chose. Imagine that things did not go well. Ask yourself the following questions:

- What is the feeling that I have right now? How did I get to this feeling?

- What was I thinking before and during the situation?

- What did I say/not say?

- What was I feeling physically before and during the situation?

- What was the main decision or attitude that got me here?

- What else do I notice about what happened?

Now let that image go. Give your body a bit of a shake and then settle back into a relaxed position again. Remember, you are imagining that the event has already happened. This time you are feeling good because things went really well. Ask yourself the following questions:

- Exactly what is the 'good' feeling that I have now? How did I get to this feeling?

- What was I thinking before and during the situation?

- What did I say/not say?

- What was I feeling physically before and during the situation?

- What was the main decision or attitude that got me here?

- What else do I notice about what happened?

When you have explored the positive future image, allow the image to fade and sit quietly for a moment, taking time to think about any insights you may have gained.

11.5 Being effective (continued)

So, the important points are:

- You don't just explore what you *don't* want – you try to be as clear as possible in working out what it is that you *do* want.

- You identify the specific things that you will do or say in order to achieve this.

- You identify any evidence that confirms your success. For example, if your goal is to feel more confident with a particular group of people you could judge your achievement by saying more than normal or by being in the group without feeling physical symptoms of anxiety.

Just one last point. You may decide at the end of this that your original goal doesn't really feel right for you anymore. Sometimes when we can see what the possible outcome could be we might decide that it isn't as great as we thought and actually we need to change it slightly (or a lot!). As long as our reasons for altering the goal are based on sound judgement and not on anxiety, we can simply go through the process again with our altered perspectives and work out what is right for us.

Have a go now at defining a goal for yourself and going through the imagery exercise outlined on the previous page. When you have finished, write down the key points that you decide on.

11.6 Summary

What I understand about the process of setting goals:

What I understand about my own goal-setting:

My positive intention is:

As you build a healthy level of self-esteem you will be increasingly able to cope with temporary setbacks and still maintain a sense of wellbeing. In the final part of this course you will have the opportunity to review what you have learnt and to decide what action you will take to sustain the changes that you are making.

Section 12

Keeping It All Going!

Aims of this section

- to review the course
- to identify resources for the future
- to celebrate achievements

12.1 A REVIEW OF BELIEFS, THOUGHTS AND ACTIONS (PAGE 252)

Participants mark the ones they feel they are still working on or need to remind themselves about. You could also revisit the 'hopes' in a pot drawing if you used this at the start of the course (see facilitator's notes for activity sheet 1.5); and/or the personal checklists (see activity sheet 2.6).

12.2 SUSTAINING THE CHANGES (PAGE 253)

Successful self-prompts might be charts on the wall, reminders on the mirror, notes on the desk at work, drawings or images made during the course or small figures of images (I have used plastic animals, for example).

12.3 COPING WITH SETBACKS (PAGE 254) AND
12.4 WHAT WORKS FOR YOU? (PAGE 255)

Both these activities are also useful for a follow-up session once the group members have had a chance to 'go it alone' for a while.

12.5 FEELING INSPIRED? (PAGE 256)

You could either take in a collection of sayings for people to choose from or set this as a task for the group to do before the last session. I also like to ask group members to bring in any other relevant literature, course information, website addresses, and so on, that they think might be interesting for the rest of the group to know about.

12.6 LETTER FROM THE EXPERT (PAGE 257)

If appropriate for the group that you are running you may want to provide stamped envelopes and offer to post these letters to participants at some point in the future. Leave at least two to three weeks before sending them.

12.7 FINISHING THE COURSE (PAGE 258)

Allow time for people to complete this during the session and still leave enough time for your closing circle and end of course celebration. The closing circle could be a time when participants are given the opportunity to say something in the group that they feel they really 'need' to say but haven't said yet, such as 'Thank you' to another group member, something important about themselves that they have discovered and want to share with the group, or something that they feel proud of achieving.

There are many 'end of course' activities that you could use during the closing circle and I am sure that you will have, or will discover, your own favourites. Here are two that I have used and have found to be effective:

- At the end of the course ask each participant to write a short 'appreciation' for everyone else. This is simply done by having one piece of paper for each person passed around the group. I have found that appreciations can be more meaningful and personal than asking members to praise each other. For example 'I really appreciate the support that you gave me when we worked together' or 'I appreciate your courage and determination in working on your goals' might be absorbed into the self-concept more easily than 'You are good at supporting others' or 'Well done for tackling your goals', both of which could sound quite patronizing. Participants read the sheet before they leave but you could also offer to add them to each person's letter from the expert. It can be a great boost to receive this sort of feedback a few weeks after the course has finished.

- As an alternative, where I have used a lot of imagery throughout a course I like to finish with an image. The group members are invited to imagine that there is a large gift box in the middle of the floor and they can take away a gift from the whole group experience. They dip their hands into the box and allow the first image that comes to mind to be their gift. Sometimes it's a word or phrase (e.g. 'increased confidence'); sometimes it's an object, animal or colour ('a deckchair to help me to relax', 'a lion for courage', 'a blue blanket to remind me of all the support I have had'). One group that had gelled particularly well chose to give the gifts to each other.

A more 'high energy' activity might be appropriate for some groups, in which case you could use something fast and simple like a Mexican wave or passing a 'high five' around the circle.

Now that the course has finished sit back, relax and reflect for a while. You deserve some time for you!

Keeping It All Going!

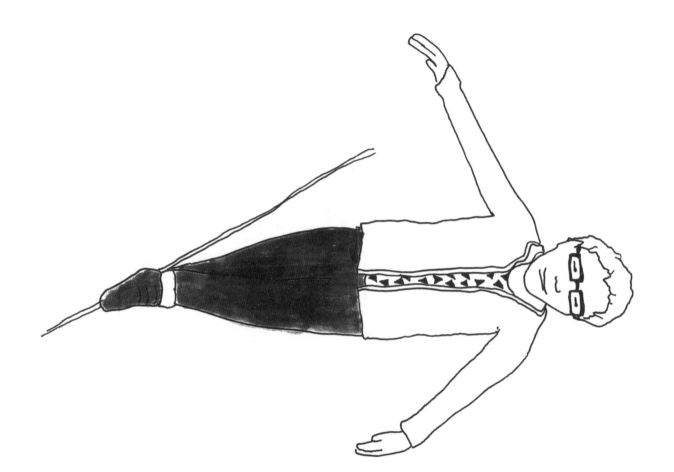

12.1 A review of beliefs, thoughts and actions

Helpful	Unhelpful
Have a mixture of long-, medium- and short-term goals for yourself. These are realistic and achievable.	Set unrealistic targets for yourself. Only set yourself long-term goals.
Self-praise is unqualified (that was a difficult situation and I handled it well).	Use qualifiers when self-praising (I handled that well. Why can't I always do that?).
Notice times when you are feeling OK, however brief or lengthy.	Only give attention to how you are feeling when there is a 'problem'.
Notice small achievements and comment positively to yourself. How do you know that you have done something well?	Only notice your big achievements. Be vague about how you know that you've done something well.
Be precise in describing your aim (While I am talking to Alan I will keep my shoulders relaxed and concentrate on listening to what he is saying).	Be vague or too general about your desired aim (I need to be more confident).
When self-evaluating, use non-judgemental words like 'difficult and 'easy'.	Use 'labels' about yourself such as 'shy', 'clumsy', 'useless'. Use judgemental words to describe your actions like 'terrible'.
Use 'I' statements (I feel upset).	Use 'they' statements (they're always making me upset).
Acknowledge the feelings behind your actions. Work out how you might have behaved differently in response to the same feeling.	Deny or make light of your feelings. Tell yourself that you can't change the way you react to difficult people and situations.
Be clear and consistent about your needs ('I am going to have some quiet time in my room to do a relaxation session').	Be inflexible about personal 'rules' that are no longer useful (I have to wait for everyone else to go out before I can relax).
Recognize your current abilities and be prepared to set yourself challenges and take small risks.	Be over-protective of yourself (I can't speak to that new person because I would feel uncomfortable). Be over-critical of yourself (I never have anything interesting to say to anyone).
Aim for imaginative problem-solving.	Blame yourself. Make the problem out to be unimportant.
Be honest with yourself. Be prepared to admit your own mistakes.	Avoid confronting your mistakes.
Use positives ('keep eye contact').	Use negatives ('don't look away').

12.2 Sustaining the changes

In taking responsibility for building your self-esteem you have made the most important step in achieving your goals. You have been able to look at where you are in life and where you want to be in the way that any scientist might begin to look at a difficulty to be solved. You, the scientist, now have the chance to continue to experiment. You may find that you need to reform some of your hypotheses because they are no longer valid but that can lead to very positive changes.

Even when we know what we want to do that doesn't necessarily mean that we will remember to do it! You may want to use as many different self-prompts as you can come up with. Think about how you already remind yourself to do things. What works best for you? Could you use any ideas that other people have come up with?

What self-prompts
am I using
successfully?

12.3 Coping with setbacks

You will be able to maintain your progress if you truly believe that what you are doing is relevant, that you are capable of doing it and that the end results are worth the effort.

You are, of course, likely to continue to come across difficult situations. Temporary setbacks may occur but, having strengthened your self-esteem, you will find it easier to learn from the experience and move on. Remember, if you can't change the situation then you will find that thinking about that situation in a different way can help you to come up with an effective coping strategy. This in turn will have a positive effect on your confidence.

For example, you may find that some people still react to you as though you had not changed. Or they may remark on your increased confidence but still be expecting you to revert to your old ways. They may continue to assume responsibility for things that you now feel capable of doing for yourself. Many people have found their progress unwittingly hampered by well-meaning friends and relatives. This will not happen, however, if you can maintain an assertive response to any attempts to draw you back into your old habits.

Devise an assertive response to a friend who has made a decision on your behalf.

Gradually, most people will adapt to the new you and if you share your adventures and changes with them you will help them to feel included rather than excluded.

12.4 What works for you?

Write down ten things that you will do in order to feel more in control of your life. Be as inventive as you can. Write them down quickly without taking too long to think about them.

1.

2.

3.

4.

5.

6.

7.

8.

9.

10.

Discuss your list with one other person. Now add five more things that you will do.

1.

2.

3.

4.

5.

Resolve to start one of these things today!

12.5 Feeling inspired?

Collect (or invent) ten motivational sayings that really appeal to you.

1.

2.

3.

4.

5.

6.

7.

8.

9.

10.

12.6 Letter from the expert

Perhaps you have made quite a few changes in the way that you think about yourself and others during this course.

Knowing all that you know now, and recognizing the progress that you have made, imagine that you are writing a letter of advice to yourself – things that you would like to remind yourself about in the future. Write anything that comes to mind. Make it as long or as brief as you want.

Put the letter in an envelope and seal it. Address it to yourself! Perhaps it will be just the thing to give you a boost at some point in the future!

12.7 Finishing the course

What are your feelings as you come to the end of your course? What do you feel confident about? What would you like to know more about?

What do you feel you have achieved during this course?

What obstacle(s) have you already overcome?

What do you think are the most important goals for you in the future?

Relaxation Exercises

1. Progressive relaxation

The technique of tensing and relaxing different muscle groups and noticing the different sensations was developed by Edmund Jacobson in the 1930s and is still widely used (Jacobsen 1938). For full benefit this is best done lying down with your arms resting by your sides.

Make yourself comfortable and close your eyes. Spend a few moments just listening to your breathing and feeling the air go in and out of your body... in and out like waves on the sea shore... You're going to feel what it's like to tighten up different parts of your body and then to relax.

When you are ready, very gradually curl your toes so that you can feel them getting tight or tense... hold that tightness for a moment... and let go. Feel the difference between what it was like to be tense and what it's like to be relaxed... Now do that again... curl your toes... feel the tension... and let go.

Now, keeping your heels on the ground, bend both your feet up towards your head. Feel the tightness in your legs when you do this. Hold it... and let go... Feel the difference... Do that once more.

Now think about the top half of your legs... tighten the muscles in the top half of your legs so that you are slightly pushing yourself up from the floor or bed... Really feel the tension... Now relax. Do that once more... Let all the tension flow out. Your legs will roll outwards when they are relaxed. Check how this feels. Notice the difference between what it feels like when your muscles are tense and when they are relaxed. Your legs will begin to feel warm and heavy.

Now think about your back. Slightly arch your back away from the floor or bed... Hold still... and then relax... Do that once more.

Tighten your stomach muscles by pulling your stomach in towards your back… Again hold this for a moment…and then gently let go with a sigh… Now push your stomach muscles outwards. Check how this feels… Let go… Repeat this once more – first pulling your stomach in…relaxing…and then pushing your stomach outwards…and relaxing again. Make sure that your legs and feet haven't tensed up again while you've been doing this.

Now you're going to move to your hands and arms. Stretch your arms out and feel which muscles you are using… Hold them stiff for a moment… Now let those muscles go floppy and heavy… Do that once more… Now gently curl your fingers until you can feel the tightness…let go and feel the difference… Now stretch your fingers out and see how that feels… Do both of those things again, curling and stretching your fingers… Let your hands rest lightly by your side now. All the tightness has gone and your arms and hands feel warm and heavy.

Think about your shoulders. Very gradually and gently raise your shoulders towards your ears. Feel what that's like… See if you feel more tightness on one side than the other… Let go gently… Now let go even more than you thought you could… Do this once more… Raise your shoulders towards your ears…hold the tightness…and let go. And now let go even more.

Now think about your neck. Slowly and gently drop your head towards one shoulder, just far enough to feel the pull of the muscles on the other side… Now slowly move your head back to the middle…and now over to the other side. Feel the tension in your muscles…and now gently back to the middle again. Check that you feel comfortable. If not, try doing that again.

Now gently close your back teeth together. Hold them closed very lightly… and let go. Press your lips together firmly and then let go… Press your tongue against the roof of your mouth and again let go… Your tongue is now resting on the floor of your mouth, your teeth are slightly apart and your lips are resting lightly together.

Think about your eyes. Close your eyes even more tightly than they already are… Now let go again… Feel the difference. Raise your eyebrows as though you were surprised…let go… Now frown and feel which muscles you are using…and relax.

Now wrinkle your nose…and let go.

Now instead of thinking of yourself in parts, feel your whole body relaxing, sinking into the floor. With each breath you are breathing out the tightness and breathing in relaxation. Feel the breath go in through your nose, down through your windpipe and into your lungs. Feel it filling your lungs… Feel your breath as the air leaves your lungs and travels out through your nose. Just notice your breathing for a while. Let it happen naturally but feel the flow of air. With each breath out you will feel more relaxed…and more calm… You will feel warm and perhaps a little sleepy. If thoughts come into your head just let them pass through then go back to feeling your breathing. Notice how your body feels different now. Enjoy this feeling for a few minutes.

When you are ready gently start to move your fingers and toes. Very gently rock from side to side just a little bit… Have a yawn and a stretch… Open your eyes gently and get used to the room again… Bend your knees and roll over onto your side before slowly sitting up.

2. Focusing

This type of relaxation works by focusing the mind on different areas of the body and just being aware of what that area of the body feels like. It is a version of the focusing exercise (activity sheet 4.1). It can be done lying down or seated. Quite often if we try to relax, we try too hard! In our efforts to relax we actually set up more tension. By observing what the body is doing there is a natural tendency to simply allow any areas of tension to relax and release. This is an exercise commonly taught as part of mindfulness meditation. It is a good exercise to do when you find your thoughts getting caught up in worries, plans and concerns.

Let your eyes close gently and settle yourself into a comfortable position. Think about your right foot and just notice what it feels like. It might be warm or cold. It might be numb or itchy. Just notice whatever you can feel…

Now think about the lower part of your right leg. Let your attention leave your right foot and just move very easily to your right leg. Notice whatever feeling is there just at this moment…

Now move up to your knee and the upper half of your right leg and notice whatever feeling is there…

Now to your right hand. Feel what's happening in your right hand…

Now think about the lower part of your right arm and feel what's happening there… Whatever is there, just notice it…

Now do the same with the upper part of your right arm. Remember there are no right or wrong feelings. Whatever you can feel is OK…

Go across your body now to the upper part of your left arm…

Now down through your elbow to the lower half of your left arm…

And now your left hand and fingers…

Now the upper half of your left leg, notice whatever is happening there…

And the lower half of your left leg…

And now down into your left foot…

Now notice both your legs and both your feet at the same time…

Now your arms and hands as well as your legs and feet…

Start to listen to whatever sounds there are around you…

When you feel ready, open your eyes and look around you. Lie or sit quietly for a short while before stretching and slowly getting up…

3. A 'calm down' relaxation

This is based on an exercise by Jane Madders, physiotherapist and teacher of health education and relaxation training (Madders 1987). In panic situations, breathing tends to become shallow and fast. If you can learn to take charge early on and bring your breathing back under your control this will help you to regain a feeling of calm more easily. For this quick relaxation to be effective you should already have experienced more detailed methods.

As soon as you notice yourself getting tense or worried say to yourself 'Be calm'.

Focus on your hands as you breathe in (this doesn't have to be a big deep breath, just normal breathing) and, as you breathe out very slowly, allow your hands to relax. On the next breath focus on your shoulders and as you breathe out allow your shoulders to relax. Finally focus on your jaw and allow your jaw to relax as you slowly breathe out. After two or three more calm breaths continue what you were doing.

Breath Control Exercises

1. Energizing breath

- Sit upright in a high backed chair so that your body is well supported and relaxed.

- Breathe naturally for a while, just feeling the rhythm of your breath.

- After a few breaths, press your left nostril closed with your thumb and inhale through your right nostril. Keep the natural rhythm of your breath.

- Release your thumb; close your right nostril with your forefinger and exhale through your left nostril.

- Without changing fingers, inhale through your left nostril.

- Change fingers. Exhale through the right nostril.

- Inhale through the right and exhale through the left and so on. Repeat the whole sequence ten times.

2. Extending exhalation

- Sit erect and well supported; your chest and head in a straight line; shoulders slightly back; hands resting easily in your lap.

- Inhale slowly as you silently count to three (one...and...two...and...three). Remember to breathe from your diaphragm.

- Hold for the count of three.

- Exhale slowly through your nostrils, counting to six.

- Count to three again before inhaling.

- Continue for about three minutes.

The reason for making the outbreath longer than the inbreath is that breathing in involves muscle contraction and the heart speeds up slightly. Breathing out involves relaxation of the muscles and the heart slows down slightly. The duration of the outbreath can be slowly increased as you practise this until you are exhaling for the count of 15 or more. The important thing is to feel the rhythm rather than to try to increase the capacity too far.

3. Combining breath control and imagery

Sit comfortably in an upright position.

Imagine that you are the yolk inside an egg and that between the yolk and the egg are seven other layers. As you breathe in imagine that you are breathing up the back of your body from the ankles to the top of your head. Pause for the count of three. Then as you breathe out, breathe down the front of your body, sweeping under your feet. Repeat this six more times, remembering the next time you breathe in to imagine that you have moved slightly further away from your body into the next level so that when you reach the seventh inbreath you are sweeping a wide circle around your body. Really let go each time you breathe out, releasing the tension from your body. Take your time with this. There is no need to rush it.

Now the next time you breathe in, breathe up the right side of your body from the feet to the top of your head and down the left hand side of your body as you breathe out. Again, do this in a circular movement sweeping under your feet and moving away from your body in a circle that gets bigger and bigger with each breath. Do this for seven breaths, remembering to pause after breathing in each time.

Exploring the Self-Esteem Approach to Wellbeing

Within the self-esteem model outlined in Part I, Chapter 1, 'Self-Esteem and Wellbeing' there are five core abilities which are key to effective change. These are: self-control, adaptability, effective observation, effective listening and imagination.

Self-control

This includes the ability to have some control over our feelings and thoughts and the ways in which we express them, the ability to tolerate waiting and manage impulsivity, the ability to consciously switch attention from one stimulus to another by choice, and the ability to persevere with difficult tasks.

Adaptability

This involves the ability to adapt to new situations and changes in contexts; the ability to monitor and adjust actions, feelings and thoughts according to realistic assessments of personal progress; and the ability to adapt to obstacles and challenges, such as a demanding listening environment. Adaptability not only enables us to move from one focus of attention to another appropriately, but also allows us to attend to more than one stimulus at the same time.

Effective listening

This includes the ability to really hear what others are saying and to reflect on what is heard. Effective listening inevitably includes self-control, for example the ability to focus on what is being said by others without allowing our own thoughts to dominate.

Effective observation

This includes the ability to observe, and to reflect on, details within our environment, non-verbal aspects of interactions and our own behaviour. It also includes the ability to expand our awareness of the main object of our attention in order to take in contextual information.

Imagination

The ability to imagine is an important aspect of learning, creativity and problem-solving. It is also vital for empathy: the ability to see things from another person's point of view and to be aware of others' needs. Imagination allows us to be more effective in directing our attention both internally (to images, feelings and thoughts) and externally. Imagination is the key to effective change (see Part I, Chapter 3, 'Working with Imagery and the Imagination').

Specific skills

Specific skills refer to the behaviours which, in effect, demonstrate the core abilities. The key concept here is *appropriateness* – the application of skills in an appropriate way. For example, in relation to the core ability of being able to control impulsivity I may need to develop skills of:

- self-rewarding

- making appropriate choices

- monitoring physical sensations

- monitoring my internal 'chatter'

- pausing and focusing on a specific stimulus (for example, focusing on my breathing).

In relation to the core ability of being able to *adapt* to a demanding listening environment that requires increased focus of attention any or all of the following specific skills may be utilized:

- problem-solving skills such as linking cause and effect, trying out different strategies, choosing and rejecting strategies appropriately

- appropriate use of requests such as asking for repetition of an instruction

- monitoring and changing posture appropriately in order to observe/ hear more effectively

- negotiating with others to facilitate turn-taking and thereby reduce distractions

- utilizing a personally effective strategy such as moving to sit nearer to the speaker.

Interconnections between the different foundation elements, abilities and skills

For me, one of the important considerations in developing and using this model (and one of the challenges) was the recognition of the interconnection between the different parts. Whichever area we are working on – specific skills, core abilities or foundation elements – we will see repercussions in the other two aspects as well. So, for example, if we can identify current efficacy in one or more of the *foundation elements* (such as self-knowledge and self-reliance) and consciously develop other foundation elements (such as self-expression) this will support us in learning and sustaining *specific skills* (such as self-monitoring of unhelpful thoughts); if we learn *specific skills* then we can directly affect our perceptions of our *core abilities* and of our strengths within the *foundation elements*; and if we identify and further develop *core abilities* (such as the ability to use the imagination constructively) we will be 'feeding' the *foundation elements*.

Similarly, there are interconnections *within* the three different aspects: when working in the domain of one of the foundation elements we will invariably see effects in other elements too; core abilities will develop alongside each other; and working on developing and improving specific skills will lead to the enhancement of others. We will see the most profound effect if we specifically structure our support with conscious awareness of these interconnections.

The interconnectedness between different aspects of the model can be illustrated by looking at how a person might cope with stress (such as the potential stresses faced by someone with low self-esteem). For example, in order to be able to make effective choices and increase our resilience to stress, we will undoubtedly need to have a well-developed level of self-awareness and self-confidence. Self-knowledge and self-acceptance and 'self and others' would also be important exploration points, since our choice of coping strategy is strongly influenced by personal temperament and past experiences, and also by environment and social support.

The core abilities of control, adaptability and effective listening and observation will all facilitate our use of appropriate coping strategies but, within different foundation elements, we may choose to develop specific skills to enhance the process (such as learning a particular stress management technique).

Within this approach I see the task of the facilitator and pupil/client as being to jointly establish the nature of the intended change; to discover which foundation elements are most vulnerable and which ones the individual might, therefore, particularly want to strengthen (e.g. self-reliance, self-confidence); to find out which core abilities the client/pupil is already capitalizing on and which ones he would like to develop further (e.g. self-control, adaptability); and decide what specific skills will be used and developed in order to reach a successful outcome (e.g. assertiveness skills, problem-solving skills).

My personal way of conceptualizing the self-esteem model, outlined in this book, is as an image of a building (see Box C.1). This has proved to be useful for some of the clients and students with whom I have worked and so I will share it here.

Box C.1 An image of the self-esteem/wellbeing model

Imagine that you and I have been invited to join a new community of wellbeing. We are offered adjoining plots and told that we can build a home within this plot, containing eight rooms (each of these rooms represents one of the self-esteem/wellbeing foundation elements).

We are told that we can have walls between the rooms or we can have a more 'open plan' design if we like, with rooms flowing into each other.

In order to complete our new homes to our desired specifications we will be given help from the current inhabitants of Wellbeing Town (representing ideas gained from reading self-help books, attending courses, talking to friends, engaging in therapy, etc.). We also need some 'core abilities' such as the ability to imagine, the ability to observe and listen effectively, a degree of self-control and the ability to adapt to different environments. The furnishings and fixtures of our two homes are likely to be different although we might naturally share some items in common. The furnishings and fixtures represent the specific skills that demonstrate and enhance our core abilities.

We can also have any number of windows and doors to facilitate views and access to and from different rooms and to and from the outside world. These represent our levels of self-efficacy and mutuality.

We each construct our homes, and move in as soon as possible. Soon, I notice that you appear to be having a lot more fun than me in your new home! You help me to realize that two of my rooms need changing. 'Beyond self' is small and sparsely furnished and the adjacent 'self-reliance' room looks more like a fortress than the relaxing, comfortable space that I would like it to be. You help me to recognize that different rooms serve important functions at different stages in our lives. I knock down a wall, shift a bit of furniture, add some comfortable floor cushions (develop a new skill) and lo and behold I have a meditation room, large enough for friends to use as well.

(Plummer 2013, pages 346–347)

Following a training session in which I presented this image to a group of students on a health studies course, 'S' chose to draw her own version of the image in her personal log. With her permission, the notes that she made to accompany her plan are given below with my comments and descriptions of her drawing given in brackets:

I found the wellbeing [self-esteem] model really interesting, especially the idea of drawing a house with rooms related to the different aspects... The first thing to notice is that it [the exercise] ended up working, and that it definitely represents me and my life at the moment... It highlighted to me that although I have quite a lot of self-confidence, I do not necessarily have the skills to portray my confidence to others... **Self-knowledge** [large room with a representation of a family tree in it]: My family tree is my life story and facilitates my self-knowledge. **Self and others** [small room containing a large X, interconnecting with rooms of self-expression and self-reliance]: I have difficulties with friendships, making this room small. My **self-acceptance** varies, sometimes it is high, other times it is low [represented by a wavy line]. I am very **self-reliant** but do not let others in [the self-reliance room has a thick wall]. [this room is] linked with 'self and others' because I want to let others in. **Self-expression:** very, very small. I find it difficult to express who I am, linked with difficulties in self and others. **Self-confidence:** I am confident, but do not have the skills to use this confidence [an empty room]. **Self-awareness:** the only room where everything is good [contains shapes of different colours]. I am self-aware and have the skills to facilitate this. **Beyond self:** I am mindful that I need to alter different areas of my self.

In this example 'S' wanted to strengthen her 'self and others' and self-expression elements. She might, perhaps, do this by further developing the core ability of adapting to new situations and by developing specific self-monitoring skills. Although she felt that she is self-confident, she identified that she would like to enhance her skills so that she could convey this confidence to others. Identification of these skills, as she sees them, could be a potential starting point for change.

Whatever our self-esteem/wellbeing homes look like at any given time they will inevitably continue to alter, sometimes in subtle ways, sometimes more dramatically, as we cope with life's ups and downs.

References

Ainsworth, M.D.S., Bell, S.M.V. and Stayton, D.J. (1971) 'Individual Differences in Strange Situation Behaviour of One-year-olds.' In H.R. Schaffer (ed.) *The Origins of Human Social Relations*. New York: Academic Press.

Bandura, A. (1971) *Social Learning Theory*. Englewood Cliffs, NJ: Prentice-Hall.

Bandura, A. (1977) 'Self-efficacy: Toward a unifying theory of behaviour change.' *Psychological Review 84*, (2), 191–215.

Benson, H. (1975) *The Relaxation Response*. New York: William Morrow.

Berg, I.K. and de Shazer, S. (1993) 'Making Numbers Talk: Language in Therapy.' In S. Friedman (ed.) *The New Language of Change: Constructive Collaboration in Psychotherapy*. New York: Guilford Press.

Bowlby, J. (1969) *Attachment and Loss. Volume 1: Attachment*. London: The Hogarth Press and The Institute of Psychoanalysis.

Burns, R.B. (1979) *The Self Concept in Theory, Measurement, Development and Behaviour*. New York: Longman.

California Task Force to Promote Self-Esteem and Personal and Social Responsibility (1990) *Toward a State of Self-esteem*. Sacramento, CA: California State Department of Education.

Casement, P. (1990) *Further Learning from the Patient: The Analytic Space and Process*. London: Tavistock/Routledge.

Cox, M. and Theilgaard, A. (1987) *Mutative Metaphors in Psychotherapy: The Aeolian Mode*. London and New York: Tavistock Publications.

Dalton, P. and Dunnett, G. (1990) *A Psychology for Living: Personal Construct Theory for Professionals and Clients*. Self-published: Dunton Publishing.

Durham, C. (2006) *Chasing Ideas*. London: Jessica Kingsley Publishers.

Eliot, L. (1999) *What's Going on in There? How the Brain and Mind Develop in the First Five Years of Life*. New York: Bantam.

Ferrucci, P. (1982) *What We May Be*. London: The Aquarian Press.

Gerhardt, S. (2004) *Why Love Matters: How Affection Shapes a Baby's Brain*. London: Routledge.

Glosser, G. and Goodglass, H. (1990) 'Disorders in executive control functions among aphasic and other brain damaged patients.' *Journal of Clinical and Experimental Neuropsychology 12*, (4), 485–501.

Glouberman, D. (2003) *Life Choices, Life Changes: Develop Your Personal Vision with Imagework* (revised edition). London: Hodder and Stoughton. (First published by Unwin Hyman 1989).

Goleman, D. (1996) *Emotional Intelligence: Why it can Matter More than IQ.* London: Bloomsbury.

Greenier, K.D., Kernis, M.H. and Waschull, S.B. (1995) 'Not All High (or Low) Self-esteem People are the Same. Theory and Research on Stability of Self-esteem.' In M.H. Kernis (ed.) *Efficacy, Agency, and Self-Esteem*. New York and London: Plenum Press.

Harper, J.F. and Marshall, E. (1991) 'Adolescents' problems and their relationship to self-esteem.' *Adolescence 26*, (104), 799–807.

Harter, S. (1999) *The Construction of the Self.* New York: Guilford Press.

Hillman, J. (1990) 'Imaginal Practice.' In T. Moore (ed.) *The Essential James Hillman: A Blue Fire.* London: Routledge.

Jacobsen, E. (1938) *Progressive Relaxation.* Chicago: University of Chicago Press.

Johnson, R.A. (1989) *Inner Work: Using Dreams and Active Imagination for Personal Growth.* New York: HarperSanFrancisco.

Jung, C.G. (ed.) (1978) *Man and His Symbols.* London: Pan Books (first published by Aldus Books Ltd, 1964).

Kabat-Zinn, J. (1996) *Full Catastrophe Living: How to Cope with Stress, Pain and Illness Using Mindfulness Meditation.* London: Piatkus.

Kelly, G.A. (1955) *The Psychology of Personal Constructs.* New York: Norton.

Madders, J. (1987) *Stress and Relaxation.* (3rd edition) London: Macdonald Optima.

Main, M. and Solomon, J. (1990) 'Procedures for Identifying Infants as Disorganised/Disorientated During the Ainsworth Strange Situation.' In M. Greenberg, D. Cicchetti and M. Cummings (eds) *Attachment During the Preschool Years: Theory, Research and Intervention.* Chicago: University of Chicago Press.

Miller, W.R. and Rollnick, S. (2002) *Motivational Interviewing: Preparing People for Change* (2nd edn). New York: Guilford Press.

Moore, T. (1992) *Care of the Soul: How to Add Depth and Meaning to Your Everyday Life.* London: Piatkus.

Nunn, K., Hanstock, T. and Lask, B. (2008) *Who's Who of the Brain.* London: Jessica Kingsley Publishers.

Overholser, J.C., Adams, D.M, Lehnert, K.L. and Brinkman, D.C. (1995) 'Self-esteem deficits and suicidal tendencies among adolescents.' *Journal of the American Academy of Child and Adolescent Psychiatry 34, 7*, 919–928.

Plummer, D. (2013) 'Stammering, Imagework and Self-esteem.' In C. Cheasman, R. Everard and S. Simpson (eds) *Stammering Therapy from the Inside: New Perspectives on Working with Young People and Adults.* Guildford: J&R Press Ltd.

Rayner, E. (1993) *Human Development: An Introduction to the Psychodynamics of Growth, Maturity and Ageing.* London: Routledge.

Rogers, C. (1961) *On Becoming a Person: A Therapist's View of Psychotherapy.* London: Constable.

Rogers, C. (1969) *Freedom to Learn: A View of What Education Might Become.* Columbus, OH: Merrill.

Saphire-Bernstein, S., Way, B.M., Kim, H.S., Sherman, D.K. and Taylor, S.E. (2011) Oxytocin receptor gene (OXTR) is related to psychological resources. *PNAS (Proceedings of the National Academy of Sciences of the United States of America)* 108, 37.

Satir, V. (1991) *Peoplemaking.* London: Souvenir Press.

Storr, A. (1989) *Solitude.* London: Fontana.

Sunderland, M. (2006) *The Science of Parenting.* London: Dorling Kindersley.

Tart, C. (1994) *Living the Mindful Life: A Handbook for Living in the Present Moment.* Boston, MA: Shambhala Publications Inc.

Zukav, G. (1991) *The Seat of the Soul.* London: Rider.

Subject Index

Author Index

Activities Index

Information Sheet Index